Cambridge Elements

Elements in Child Development
edited by
Marc H. Bornstein
National Institute of Child Health and Human Development, Bethesda
Institute for Fiscal Studies, London
UNICEF, New York City

STRESS IN CHILDHOOD

Camelia E. Hostinar
University of California, Davis

Anna M. Parenteau
University of California, Davis

Geneva M. Jost
University of California, Davis

Sally Hang
University of California, Davis

Joanna Y. Guan
University of California, Davis

Jamie M. Lawler
Eastern Michigan University

Shaftesbury Road, Cambridge CB2 8EA, United Kingdom

One Liberty Plaza, 20th Floor, New York, NY 10006, USA

477 Williamstown Road, Port Melbourne, VIC 3207, Australia

314–321, 3rd Floor, Plot 3, Splendor Forum, Jasola District Centre, New Delhi – 110025, India

103 Penang Road, #05–06/07, Visioncrest Commercial, Singapore 238467

Cambridge University Press is part of Cambridge University Press & Assessment, a department of the University of Cambridge.

We share the University's mission to contribute to society through the pursuit of education, learning and research at the highest international levels of excellence.

www.cambridge.org
Information on this title: www.cambridge.org/9781009644440

DOI: 10.1017/9781009420228

© Camelia E. Hostinar, Anna M. Parenteau, Geneva M. Jost, Sally Hang, Joanna Y. Guan, and Jamie M. Lawler 2025

This publication is in copyright. Subject to statutory exception and to the provisions of relevant collective licensing agreements, no reproduction of any part may take place without the written permission of Cambridge University Press & Assessment.

When citing this work, please include a reference to the DOI 10.1017/9781009420228

First published 2025

A catalogue record for this publication is available from the British Library

ISBN 978-1-009-64444-0 Hardback
ISBN 978-1-009-42024-2 Paperback
ISSN 2632-9948 (online)
ISSN 2632-993X (print)

Cambridge University Press & Assessment has no responsibility for the persistence or accuracy of URLs for external or third-party internet websites referred to in this publication and does not guarantee that any content on such websites is, or will remain, accurate or appropriate.

For EU product safety concerns, contact us at Calle de José Abascal, 56, 1°, 28003 Madrid, Spain, or email eugpsr@cambridge.org

Stress in Childhood

Elements in Child Development

DOI: 10.1017/9781009420228
First published online: October 2025

Camelia E. Hostinar
University of California, Davis

Anna M. Parenteau
University of California, Davis

Geneva M. Jost
University of California, Davis

Sally Hang
University of California, Davis

Joanna Y. Guan
University of California, Davis

Jamie M. Lawler
Eastern Michigan University

Author for correspondence: Camelia E. Hostinar, cehostinar@ucdavis.edu

Abstract: The innocence of childhood does not protect against exposure to stress. More than half of US children experience adversities, such as abuse, neglect, witnessing domestic violence, parental psychopathology, or divorce, and all children encounter normative stressors like school transitions and challenges with peers. This Element discusses research on stress psychobiology during childhood, from birth to age 10. The Element focuses on important contexts that shape children's responses to stress and their coping capacities, including the family system, peers, schools, neighborhoods, the broader culture, as well as clinical settings. Sources of stress and resilience in each context are described.

Keywords: stress, childhood, resilience, adversity, review

© Camelia E. Hostinar, Anna M. Parenteau, Geneva M. Jost, Sally Hang, Joanna Y. Guan, and Jamie M. Lawler 2025

ISBNs: 9781009644440 (HB), 9781009420242 (PB), 9781009420228 (OC)
ISSNs: 2632-9948 (online), 2632-993X (print)

Contents

1 Stress in Childhood: The Mind–Body Connection   1

2 Stress and Resilience in Family Systems   14

3 Stress and Belonging in Peer Relationships   24

4 Stress and the School Environment   29

5 The Role of Neighborhoods in Stress and Resilience   36

6 Discrimination Stress and Cultural Sources of Resilience   43

7 Stress, Trauma, and Mental Health Interventions   47

8 Rearing Resilient Children   55

   References   57

1 Stress in Childhood: The Mind–Body Connection

It is always bedtime when children ask their existential questions: Why does my heart race when I am scared? Why do we have nightmares sometimes? Is there a way to live forever? Although questions like these may simply be a time-honored stalling tactic to delay sleep, children are probably also voicing their emerging anxieties as human beings grappling with the reality of having a conscious mind that has only partial control of and limited information about the body it inhabits. Once children fall asleep, their caregivers turn to each other or the internet to pose their own questions: Why is the birth of a sibling stressful for children? What treatments can help a child who has experienced stress or trauma? As caregivers drift to sleep, developmental scientists ponder similar questions: How does the psychology of stress relate to its underlying biology? What factors lead children to become more vulnerable or more resilient to stress? What explains the immense variability in individual responses to stress? How do childhood experiences shape one's later capacity to cope with stress in adulthood?

This Element grew out of our hope that providing current knowledge about stress psychobiology and the factors that shape individual differences in children's stress reactivity to scientists, practitioners, and caregivers would promote successful coping and better mental health among children. We focus on the developmental period from birth to age 10, given its foundational role in establishing starting points for future trajectories of risk and resilience. Discussing research on stress psychobiology during childhood may also serve as a guide toward fruitful avenues for intervention and may open channels of communication among scientific, practitioner, and parenting communities. Each of the following sections focuses on an important context that shapes children's responses to stress and their coping ability, including the family system (Section 2), peers (Section 3), schools (Section 4), neighborhoods (Section 5), the broader culture and children's exposure to discrimination (Section 6), as well as clinical and treatment settings (Section 7). Throughout these sections, we highlight evidence of bidirectional associations between children's stress reactivity and their socioemotional difficulties, such as the link between peer difficulties and elevated cortisol levels, which in turn predict subsequent peer difficulties, as discussed in Sections 3 and 4. Each section profiles both sources of stress and protective factors that promote resilience in each context. Resilience is defined as positive adjustment despite exposure to stress and is increasingly viewed as a process of successful adaptation when sufficient resources for coping exist rather than an individual trait contained solely within individuals (Masten, 2018). For this reason, each section will highlight protective factors that promote the process of successful adaptation. We will conclude by summarizing insights regarding children's resilience to stress in Section 8. Throughout these sections, we will highlight the myriad factors that produce individual differences in stress reactivity, leading some children to succumb and others to thrive when confronted with stressors. Understanding the developmental origins of these individual differences is critical for identifying targets for intervention and shifting developmental trajectories towards positive outcomes.

1.1 Lessons from Stress Biology

An adaptive but sometimes unpleasant feature of human experience is the stress response. When the brain detects changes in the environment that may pose a real or perceived threat to current or future well-being (such an event constitutes a *stressor*), the psychobiological stress response is activated to help us adapt (McEwen, 2007). Stress can be defined as a "real or interpreted threat to the physiological or psychological integrity of an individual that results in physiological and/or behavioral responses" (McEwen, 2000, p. 508). Stress is related to but somewhat distinct from anxiety, which entails worry about anticipated or possible threats that have yet to materialize (see Table 1 for definitions of commonly used terms in the field of stress research). When stress is particularly severe or long-lasting, it becomes "trauma" or "traumatic stress." "Toxic stress" is another related concept introduced by the National Scientific Center on the Developing Child to indicate severe stress without access to supportive relationships. In contrast, mild or brief forms of stress that can teach children coping skills (e.g., first day of school) are labeled "positive stress." Forms of stress that are more serious but temporary and manageable with support from the environment are referred to as "tolerable stress" and would not be described as trauma or traumatic stress. Distinguishing between these different terms is important for clinical practice and research.

Importantly, stress perceptions are subjective, and it is possible for the same event to be interpreted as stressful, neutral, or positive by different children. To emphasize the importance of subjective appraisal, some define stress as "the relationship between the person and the environment that is appraised by the person as taxing or exceeding his or her resources and endangering his or her well-being" (Lazarus & Folkman, 1984, p. 19). In the developmental literature, there have been calls to improve precision of stress measurement by moving beyond checklists of events and towards understanding "how various factors influence the way events are experienced by the child" (Smith & Pollak, 2020, p. 11). Theoretical proposals have also discussed the possibility of defining stress as a lack of perceived safety (rather than the presence of threat), based on

Table 1 Definitions of common terminology in the study of stress

Term	Definition	Source
Anxiety	"An emotion characterized by apprehension and somatic symptoms of tension in which an individual anticipates impending danger, catastrophe, or misfortune."	American Psychological Association (2018)
Distress	"A set of painful mental and physical symptoms that are associated with normal fluctuations of mood in most people."	American Psychological Association (2018)
Positive stress	"Brief increases in heart rate, mild elevations in stress hormone levels."	Center on the Developing Child (2024)
Stress	"A real or interpreted threat to the physiological or psychological integrity of an individual that results in physiological and/or behavioral responses."	McEwen (2000, p. 508)
Stressful life events	"Life experiences or events that may result in changes in their lives and that necessitate varying levels of coping and adaptation."	J. H. Johnson (1982, p. 219)
Tolerable stress	"Serious, temporary stress responses, buffered by supportive relationships."	Center on the Developing Child (2024)
Toxic stress	"Prolonged activation of stress response systems in the absence of protective relationships."	Center on the Developing Child (2024)
Trauma	"A frightening, dangerous, or violent event that poses a threat to a child's life or bodily integrity."	National Child Traumatic Stress Network (2024a)

neuroscientific evidence that the brain is tracking safety cues in the environment (Brosschot et al., 2017; Smith & Pollak, 2021).

One way to increase the objectivity of stress measurement is to capture physiological changes. Stressors activate the biological stress response, a set of biochemical and physiological reactions that has been largely conserved throughout evolutionary history, presumably due to the survival advantages it confers by allowing organisms to adapt their internal physiology to cope with changes in their external environment (Taborsky et al., 2022). However, a modern understanding of the stress response in humans began with Walter Cannon's (1915) examination of the anatomy and physiology of the autonomic nervous system (ANS). Cannon coined the term "fight-or-flight" to capture the behavioral tendencies exhibited by animals and humans during a stress response, launching the modern study of the effects of stress on behavior (Carter & Goldstein, 2015). Cannon's research linked the "fight-or-flight" response to the activity of the sympathetic-adrenal-medullary (SAM) system, which results in the release of adrenaline and noradrenaline from the adrenal glands and underpins the hallmark "fight-or-flight" responses such as increased heart rate, cardiac output, blood pressure, and other physiological changes that support swift reactions to threats (Carter & Goldstein, 2015). These physiological changes are coupled with subjective experiences of heightened mental alertness and a shift towards high-arousal, negative emotional states, such as fear, anxiety, anger, or aggression (Carter & Goldstein, 2015).

Several decades after Cannon's pioneering work, electrocardiography (ECG) and impedance cardiography (ICG) enabled noninvasive examination of both the sympathetic nervous system (SNS) and parasympathetic nervous system (PNS) branches of the ANS by measuring their influences on heart activity in children. This research revealed the roles of both the SNS and PNS in socioemotional development and the development of psychopathology in children (Quigley & Moore, 2018). For instance, high levels of PNS activity – the "rest-and-digest" branch of the ANS that promotes rest and relaxation – are linked to better emotion regulation and lower risk of psychopathology in children, whereas exposure to stress in childhood is linked to lower levels of parasympathetic influence on the heart at rest (Quigley & Moore, 2018). The first five years of life appear to be a key period of development and maturation for both the SNS and PNS, and their activity levels relative to each other appear to stabilize by age 5 (Quigley & Moore, 2018). This developmental pattern suggests the importance of promoting a balanced pattern of autonomic activity, with higher levels of PNS activity and lower levels of SNS activity (the "fight-or-flight" system), although more research is needed to fully characterize the environmental characteristics that promote a balanced pattern of autonomic activity.

The hypothalamic-pituitary-adrenal axis (HPA axis) is another major stress-response system. When the brain appraises a set of stimuli as a threat, it triggers a cascade starting in the paraventricular nucleus of the hypothalamus, which releases the neuropeptides corticotropin-releasing hormone (CRH) and arginine vasopressin (AVP); these neuropeptides travel to the pituitary gland and initiate the production of adrenocorticotropic hormone (ACTH), which is released into the general circulation, ultimately reaching the adrenal glands; in response, the adrenals secrete the hormone cortisol into circulation, which subsequently binds to its receptors throughout the body and the brain to have a variety of physiological and behavioral effects during stress (Gunnar et al., 2015). The role of cortisol in the stress response was first recognized by Hans Selye (1956), who popularized the term "stress" and advanced the idea of stress as a non-specific bodily response to a wide variety of challenges and threats, physical or psychological. Selye proposed the General Adaptation Syndrome (GAS), a template for a prototypical stress response that is general enough to respond to a wide range of physical and psychological threats. Selye proposed that the GAS involves three stages: initial alarm, followed by resistance to the stressor, and finally exhaustion. The exhaustion stage occurs if stressors are prolonged or inescapable, ultimately leading to the development of physical disease.

Although initially cortisol had to be measured in blood or urine, the advent of salivary cortisol assays facilitated its measurement in child development studies (Gunnar, 2021). Developmental studies have linked HPA function to multiple aspects of socioemotional development, including psychopathology (see Gunnar, 2021, for a review of major findings from four decades of research). First, studies have revealed the crucial role of caregivers who are the child's primary attachment figures in dampening his or her cortisol stress responses, a phenomenon termed the *social buffering of stress* (Gunnar & Donzella, 2002; Hostinar et al., 2014). Second, research has highlighted the role of temperament in shaping individual differences in stress reactivity (Lengua et al., 2024). For instance, children who are shy (also known as behaviorally inhibited) can exhibit higher cortisol reactivity to acute social stressors (Gunnar et al., 2015). Finally, research with children who experience chronic stress, such as ongoing maltreatment or living in institutional care without consistent caregivers, has revealed atypical or dysregulated patterns of HPA activity among these children, both while they are experiencing chronic stress and years later, after being removed from adverse circumstances (Bunea et al., 2017; Gunnar & Vazquez, 2001; McLaughlin et al., 2015). One such dysregulated pattern is hypocortisolism – that is, low or blunted cortisol production (Fries et al., 2005; Gunnar & Vazquez, 2001). Hypocortisolism has been linked to symptoms of fatigue, pain, PTSD, and immune dysregulation (Fries et al., 2005; Miller et al., 2007). Although acute stressors (i.e., that are brief and have a clear onset and offset) typically increase cortisol production by the adrenal glands (Gunnar et al., 2015), accumulating evidence suggests that chronic (i.e., persistent stressors), which likely entail chronically elevated levels of cortisol for long periods, appear to lead to a downregulation of the HPA axis to produce lower levels of cortisol (Fries et al., 2005). Indeed, studies have revealed lower cortisol reactivity among children exposed to *prolonged* periods of stress compared to those unexposed (Bunea et al., 2017; McLaughlin et al., 2015). These findings have real-world implications, as hypocortisolism can mediate the link between experiences of adversity and teacher-reported attention and externalizing problems during kindergarten (Koss et al., 2016).

Stress responses to normative challenges that resolve quickly are highly adaptive, as they provide the energy and alertness needed to cope with changes or possible threats in the environment. However, it is now well documented that chronic, prolonged and extreme forms of stress in childhood, such as ongoing abuse or neglect, lead to "wear and tear" on the brain and body, reducing the capacity to cope with future stressors and increasing risk for physical and mental illness across the lifespan (Felitti et al., 1998; McEwen & Wingfield, 2010). Whereas the ongoing process of adaptation facilitated by physiological changes is called allostasis (i.e., maintaining stability through change, Sterling & Eyer,1988; McEwen & Wingfield, 2010), the cumulative physiological "wear and tear" on the body due to chronic stress has been named allostatic load (McEwen & Wingfield, 2010). Research on allostatic load has revealed complex interactions of the HPA axis and ANS with each other and with other bodily systems, including the immune, metabolic, and cardiovascular systems, all of which can show dysregulation with exposure to chronic stress (McEwen & Wingfield, 2010). For example, cortisol has anti-inflammatory effects, playing a role in containing immune responses under normal conditions, but dysregulation of cortisol-immune interactions may lead to excessive immune responses -i.e., inflammation (Fries et al., 2005). As such, research with adults has begun using several biological indices across multiple systems to capture allostatic load, ranging from cortisol and epinephrine/norepinephrine to inflammatory markers, blood pressure, and symptoms of metabolic syndrome (Gruenewald et al., 2012). In children, allostatic load may manifest as blunted cortisol reactivity or low basal cortisol (Sumner et al., 2019), growth delay or stunting (Johnson et al., 2011), heightened activation of some aspects of immunity as reflected in inflammation markers (Bernard et al., 2019), and behavioral or psychological symptoms (Badanes et al., 2011). Accelerated aging, as indexed by DNA methylation, and precocious pubertal development are also possible markers of chronic exposure to threatening experiences and allostatic load in children (Sumner et al., 2019).

Given that chronic stress is more likely to be associated with health symptoms and problems than acute, manageable stress (Shonkoff et al., 2021), public health efforts should focus on interventions, treatments, and psychoeducational approaches that promote stress recovery and limit the duration of stress responses. As discussed in subsequent sections, social support from family and peers (Sections 2 and 3), supportive and safe school environments

(Section 4), opportunities for outdoor physical activity and access to green spaces (Section 5), culturally transmitted coping strategies (Section 6), and therapy (Section 7) are some of the most effective strategies for promoting recovery after stressors and minimizing the long-term negative consequences of chronic stress on children's health. We focus primarily on the effects of chronic stress (also known as adversity) on children's concurrent and later functioning throughout the following sections, as chronic stress is a major source of problematic mental and physical health outcomes. In contrast, acute stress is less likely to disrupt development. To facilitate the prompt recognition of signs and symptoms of chronic stress in children, researchers are making efforts to understand how biological changes in stress-response systems map onto affective, behavioral, cognitive, and somatic responses to stress.

1.2 The ABCs of Stress: Signs of Stress in Children

The stress response involves **a**ffective, **b**ehavioral, **c**ognitive, and **s**omatic components – the ABCS of stress (Hostinar et al., 2023). Decades of research have revealed widespread variability in responses to stress across individuals in the magnitude of the stress response and in the specific constellation of affective, behavioral, cognitive, and somatic symptoms individuals display in response to stress (Gilgoff et al., 2024; McEwen & Akil, 2020; Rab & Admon, 2021). Children also show widespread individual differences in stress reactivity, which are revealed when they undergo standardized laboratory stress protocols, such as public speaking tasks. These protocols often uncover both quantitative differences in the biological stress responses measured across children and qualitative differences in the affective and behavioral responses children display (Gunnar & Donzella, 2002). Individual differences in stress reactivity likely stem from many sources, including variations in environmental factors such as the quality of caregiving children receive, genetic factors, as well as gene–environment interactions (Gunnar & Donzella, 2002; McEwen & Akil, 2020; Rab & Admon, 2021). Individual differences in stress responses can be as dramatic as to elicit opposite behaviors in different individuals: Some children may respond to stress by showing externalizing problems such as aggressive behaviors (Kalvin et al., 2016), also known as "fight-or-flight" behaviors, whereas others exhibit increases in altruism and prosociality under stress, also known as "tend-and-befriend" behaviors (Alen et al., 2021; Li et al., 2013). Ongoing research is making strides to understand when, why, and how these differences across individuals emerge and how unique features of stressors may trigger different responses.

Research with pediatric samples who have experienced severe stressors reveals common signs of stress. For instance, Dowdney (2000) summarized various affective, behavioral, cognitive, and somatic responses observed in children after the death of a family member. Possible affective reactions include sadness, grief, despair, anger, fear, anxiety, guilt, loss of interest in all activities, and irritability. Children younger than 5 years old may also present with increased separation anxiety, clinginess, dependency, and nocturnal fears or nightmares.

Behaviorally, children's distress can manifest as crying, social withdrawal, tantrums, aggression, arguments with siblings, and regression in some developmental milestones (Dowdney, 2000). School refusal is also common and may be related to cognitive responses to stress (Dowdney, 2000). Teachers often report increased academic and behavioral problems among children affected by stressful life events (Dubow & Tisak, 1989), although children who have access to social support from their family, peers, or teachers and strong problem-solving skills appear to be at lower risk of experiencing these negative consequences of stress (Dubow & Tisak, 1989).

In the cognitive domain, chronic stress can have negative impacts on children's executive function skills, including working memory, inhibitory control, and cognitive flexibility (Hostinar et al., 2012; Lund et al., 2020). Despite these robust links between severe or long-term stressors and reduced cognitive performance, some studies find that children's cognitive performance is less affected or even enhanced by short-term, mild stressors, such as public speaking. For example, one study of 8- to 10-year-olds revealed no negative effects of a brief laboratory public speaking task on children's working memory (Quesada et al., 2012) and another study showed that higher cortisol responses to a public speaking task enhanced memory of the task two weeks later among 7- to 8-year-old children (Quas et al., 2013), consistent with work in adults that shows acute stress can enhance emotional memories (Schwabe et al., 2012). This body of research reveals adaptive aspects of the stress response, which facilitates future recognition of threats by enhancing memory for threatening or emotionally salient events. In summary, the literature has documented both cognitive and behavioral deficits among children exposed to long-term stressors, while showing that brief or mild stress responses can facilitate adaptation, sometimes by sharpening certain aspects of cognition.

Somatic responses to stress can involve a wide range of bodily changes, due to the energetic demands of activating the stress response and the impacts of stressful experiences on the production of numerous hormones and neurotransmitters (McEwen & Wingfield, 2010). Children can experience changes in appetite, digestion, sleep, and activity level, and may report increased fatigue and pain symptoms, including headaches and stomachaches (Dowdney, 2000). For example, children who have previous experiences of chronic stress, such as being in foster care or institutional care, often exhibit gastrointestinal symptoms that are correlated with emotional problems (Callaghan et al., 2019). Children younger than 5 may show increased bedwetting (Dowdney, 2000). Exposure to stress, particularly if chronic and severe, can also lead to somatic growth delay and growth stunting that is associated with socioemotional changes – for example, growth delay in internationally adopted children is associated with a dysregulated social behavior known as disinhibited social approach to strangers (Johnson et al., 2011). It is notable that children report more somatic complaints than parental accounts would suggest (Dowdney, 2000), implying that children may not always spontaneously share these bodily symptoms with their caregivers. Therefore, it is important to communicate with children about bodily symptoms and any physical discomfort they may be experiencing.

In response to major stressors such as the death of a parent, some children can develop symptoms that are severe enough to warrant clinical diagnoses, including depression, anxiety disorders, and even post-traumatic stress disorder (PTSD) (Dowdney, 2000). Even when they experience these disturbances, some children show significant decreases in these symptoms over a 1-year period (Dowdney, 2000). Whether children recover quickly or these tragic events create long-lasting vulnerability and clinical levels of impairment depends on many factors, including the nature, duration, and severity of the stressor, the coping resources of the child and their family at the time of the event, and the success of clinical treatments or interventions, among other factors (Alen et al., 2024). We describe some of these connections between features or ingredients of stressful events and child outcomes next.

1.3 Which Experiences Are Stressful? The Core Ingredients of Stress

Certain dimensions or "ingredients" of experiences activate stress physiology reliably and in most children. For example, physical stressors such as pain and cold activate cortisol stress responses as early as infancy, as shown by studies examining responses to physical examinations, medical procedures like inoculations, heel lance, and venipunctures, and being cold after removal from a bath (Gunnar et al., 2009).

Threat and deprivation are two other dimensions of stressful exposures that have been repeatedly and differentially linked to negative mental health and neurodevelopmental outcomes in children (Sheridan & McLaughlin, 2014). Threat has been defined as "actual or threatened death, injury, sexual violation, or other harm to one's physical integrity" (Sheridan & McLaughlin, 2014, p. 580), whereas deprivation entails "the absence of expected cognitive and social input" (Sheridan & McLaughlin, 2014, p. 580). Accumulating evidence documents the negative consequences of both threat and deprivation for children's emotional and neurobiological development, even though each shapes development in unique ways (Machlin et al., 2019; Peverill et al., 2023).

Social stressors are some of the most common types of stressors encountered by children. A particularly potent ingredient of social stress in childhood is loss, which can involve separation from or death of an attachment figure. Even brief separations from parents can elicit a stress response in infants and toddlers, as can laboratory protocols in which parents are instructed to be non-responsive to their child (Gunnar et al., 2009). Older children are less affected by brief separations. The permanent loss of a parent or sibling can trigger serious mental health difficulties (Dowdney, 2000). Additionally, conflict and a lack of positive interactions with family members are sources of stress for children (see Section 2). Social exclusion by peers, rejection, humiliation, discrimination, and social evaluation are other dimensions of social experience that elicit stress and may portend negative mental health outcomes for children (see Sections 3 and 4).

Another dimension of stress that is gaining recognition is unpredictability, defined as variability in environmental conditions (Ellis et al., 2009; McLaughlin et al., 2021). Although defining and measuring unpredictability remains a challenge (Ugarte & Hastings, 2024), so far, researchers have focused on capturing events that cause significant change and uncertainty, such as relocations or disruptions in family structure or capturing living conditions that lack order and consistent routines. Children whose lives are more unpredictable are more reluctant to engage in exploration (Xu et al., 2023) and are at greater risk of psychopathology later in adolescence (Doom et al., 2016). Unpredictability due to inconsistency in parenting behavior appears to be particularly detrimental to children's well-being (Ugarte & Hastings, 2024).

Although similar to unpredictability, uncontrollability is a related yet distinct dimension of stress, which has been defined as an inability "to alter the intensity, duration, onset, or termination of a stressor" (Cohodes et al., 2023, p. 2288). Lack of control exacerbates the negative impacts of stressors, whereas controllability reduces their impact and promotes resilience (Cohodes et al., 2023; Maier & Watkins, 2010). An obvious application of this research is that enhancing a sense of perceived or actual control and agency may reduce the perception of stress and helplessness.

Understanding the core ingredients of stress may suggest avenues for alleviating stress in children. For example, a life event like the birth of a sibling often includes multiple ingredients of stress: loss (of time with parents), exclusion (from family interactions), unpredictability (due to changes in routines), uncontrollability (due to being unable to alter or control the course of family life), and physical stressors (e.g., sleep-interrupting noise). It is no surprise that the birth of a sibling is a potent stressor for many children. However, deconstructing such a stressful life event into its components also suggests strategies for alleviating stress. The sense of loss and exclusion may be minimized through regular one-on-one time with parents; predictability and controllability may be increased by providing the child with routine as well as some options and choices; and overall stress may be reduced by minimizing the child's exposure to physical stressors such as nighttime noise or sleep deprivation. Understanding the dimensions that underlie stressful experiences also helps inform instruments for assessing stress in children.

1.4 Stress Measures and Assessments for Children

Depending on their goals, developmental scientists and clinicians use multiple complementary strategies to assess children's perceptions of stress and exposure to stressors, their signs and symptoms of stress, and biological stress responses. Because stress is a multidimensional construct, measurement approaches can focus on various dimensions, ranging from cognitive and affective manifestations to reports regarding exposure to stressful events collected from children, parents, or teachers, as well as stress biomarkers or continuous physiological recordings.

Although the youngest children may struggle to verbalize their internal states, and "stress" is not a concept that most young children have knowledge about, children as young as 2 or 3 years show a rudimentary understanding of basic emotions, such as sadness and feeling bad (versus good). For example, they are capable of correctly stating that a character will be sad if they fail to find something they are searching for or happy if they find it (Wellman & Woolley, 1990). Later in development, 4- to 5-year-olds can predict whether someone will feel good or bad when their goals are achieved or prevented (Lagattuta, 2005). Once they reach the age of 6 or 7, children can self-report more complex states such as distress or stress. For instance, clinicians and researchers have used pictorial scales like the Subjective Units of Distress Scale (SUDS; Kiyimba & O'Reilly, 2020) to ask children as young as 6 years to indicate their level of distress or stress (or other emotions like fear or anger) by pointing to a drawing of a thermometer with levels labeled from 0 to 10 (Kiyimba & O'Reilly, 2020). Longer questionnaires like the Perceived Stress Scale for Kids (Davis & Turner-Cobb, 2023) can be used to ask school-aged children ages 7 to 11 about their stress-related perceptions and thoughts.

Beyond the subjective experience of stress, objective exposure to stressful life events as reported by parents, teachers, and children themselves can also be captured by using life events scales (Compas, 1987). One of the most widely used measures of exposure to major childhood stressors is the Adverse Childhood Experiences (ACE) Study questionnaire (Felitti et al., 1998), which asks about ten adverse experiences that forecast higher risk of later psychological and mental illness and include physical, sexual, or emotional abuse; emotional or physical neglect; witnessing domestic violence; parental substance use; parental mental illness; parental divorce or separation; or incarceration of a family member. More than half of US children experience at least one ACE. Although the questionnaire is primarily used with adolescents and adults, parental reports of child exposure to these types of events can be collected for younger children. To obtain comprehensive measures of multiple types of stressors, researchers also use semi-structured Life Stress Interviews (Rudolph & Hammen, 1999) that ask older children and their parents to describe chronic and episodic life events that occurred in the child's life during a specified time window. Finally, parents, pediatricians, and clinicians may also collect information about behavioral problems and clinical symptoms to facilitate diagnoses of stress-related disorders like PTSD, depression, and others (see Section 7 and Sege et al., 2017 for behavioral manifestations of childhood trauma and strategies for detecting them in clinical settings).

Although hormonal assays, electrophysiological recordings, and neuroimaging are frequently collected in research settings, these measures are still experimental and not yet ready to be deployed in clinical settings for diagnosing stress-related conditions or recommending specific treatments. Nevertheless, they provide valuable insights into developmental trajectories of stress responses and coping in children.

Hormonal assays often focus on cortisol, the primary hormonal output of the HPA axis, or epinephrine and norepinephrine when the goal is to capture the activity of the ANS. Salivary cortisol is the most commonly used hormonal biomarker in research settings to capture responses to acute and chronic stress in children due to the ease and non-invasive nature of saliva collection (Gunnar et al., 2015; Lynch et al., 2022). In addition to saliva, cortisol has been assessed in blood, urine, hair, and in skin, nail clippings, and tears (Lynch et al., 2022). Most measures capture short-term changes in cortisol production (from minutes to days), but hair cortisol concentration provides a cumulative metric of cortisol produced over a period of 1 to 6 months based on 1- to 6-cm-long hair samples, as hair grows approximately 1 cm per month (Meyer & Novak, 2012). Children who experience higher levels of stress exhibit higher levels of hair cortisol (Li et al., 2023), supporting the possible utility of this biomarker and potential to move from research to clinical settings in the future.

Electrophysiological recordings are also used to capture the activity of the ANS, including its sympathetic and parasympathetic branches. Measures to detect SNS activation include pre-ejection period (PEP), a measure of heart contractility derived from cardiac impedance data recorded using chest electrodes, and electrodermal activity, a measure of changes in the skin's conductance due to changes in palm sweat production, which is captured with electrodes attached to the palms (Alen et al., 2022; Mendes, 2009). PNS activity can be captured via cardiac measures such as high-frequency heart rate variability (HF-HRV), defined as the heart rate variability occurring in the respiratory frequency band (for reviews of this and other ANS indices, see Quigley & Moore, 2018; Quigley et al., 2024). These measures have been used in pediatric samples to examine the development of the ANS as well as its connections with positive or negative aspects of the social environment and the development of emotion regulation (Quigley & Moore, 2018). For instance, chronic stress in childhood has been linked to lower levels of HF-HRV at rest (Alen et al., 2022). Adults who report having experienced warmer parenting during childhood exhibit higher resting HF-HRV in midlife (Alen et al., 2020), supporting a role of warm parenting in shaping the activity of the parasympathetic nervous system (Alen et al., 2022).

Studies have also begun uncovering the neural consequences of exposure to adversity in childhood. A review of 109 neuroimaging studies revealed that children exposed to threatening experiences, such as maltreatment, tend to exhibit smaller volumes in the amygdala, medial prefrontal cortex, and hippocampus, as well as greater activity in the amygdala in response to threatening stimuli (McLaughlin et al., 2019). Fewer studies have used EEG measures to capture neural reactivity to stress, but frontal alpha asymmetry is one potentially useful biomarker, with left frontal asymmetry being linked to more externalizing problems among 5-year-old children whose families experience more daily hassles (Mulligan et al., 2022).

Researchers have also begun using wearable devices such as wristwatches to capture children's stress responses continuously for longer periods of time. Wearable technology can capture changes in stress-related physiological signals using non-invasive sensors that capture electrodermal activity, photoplethysmography, ECG, and skin temperature (Fang et al., 2022; González Ramírez et al., 2023). Although more research is needed to test their accuracy and utility in child samples, these wearable devices promise new ways to track child well-being in naturalistic environments, assist with the diagnosis of mood disorders (McGinnis et al., 2018), and provide real-time data on deviations from children's typical physiological baselines.

In summary, stress has measurable effects on children and can negatively impact their physical and mental well-being, especially if it is chronic and occurs in the absence of emotional support from close relationships, such as their family system.

2 Stress and Resilience in Family Systems

> The children stood near by, drawing figures in the dust with bare toes, and the children sent exploring senses out to see whether men and women would break. The children peeked at the faces of the men and women, and then drew careful lines in the dust with their toes.
>
> (Steinbeck, 1939, p. 6).

Children often take emotional cues from adults, synchronizing their stress responses with those of their family (Hibel et al., 2015; Lucas-Thompson & Goldberg, 2011). Family systems theory is a useful framework for understanding how family dynamics influence child functioning and views the family as a complex system (Bateson, 1972). This theory considers interdependencies within the family unit (Bowen Center for the Study of the Family, 2024) and their impact on child development. This section highlights examples of stressors that occur in the family and their impact on children's stress and coping capabilities, illustrating the family systems perspective and the cascading effects of family-level stress on children.

Developmental research has revealed numerous pathways through which families can be a source of stress or resilience for children. First, stressors affecting the family, such as economic hardship, can impact children directly or indirectly through caregiving behaviors. Second, dyadic relationships with family members can regulate child stress physiology through processes of stress spillover, stress contagion, and synchrony. Parenting behaviors and changes to the parent-child relationship can also impact the stress response. Lastly, a lack of predictability or consistent family routines may be a source of stress in children's lives. Several of these factors also impact children's resilience to stress.

2.1 Familial Sources of Stress

2.1.1 The Family Stress Model

Stressors that impact the family can influence children both directly and indirectly. For instance, financial problems are a common stressor for many families and can lead to parenting stress and parental psychological distress, which may limit the capacity for sensitive and supportive parenting behaviors toward the children (Mistry et al., 2002). The *Family Stress Model* (Conger et al., 1992; Masarik & Conger, 2017) provides evidence that economic stress has negative consequences on a family's functioning and the parent–child relationship. The family stress model proposes that children from lower socioeconomic status (SES) families may be more likely to experience harsh parenting, as parents in these families confront more stressors. Economic hardship and associated pressures can lead to parental psychological distress, which may disrupt positive parenting practices. When parents experience psychological distress, they may engage in inconsistent or harsh parenting, monitor their children less, or provide less support and affection, all of which may significantly impact children's outcomes, including self-regulation and cognitive outcomes (Masarik & Conger, 2017; Nievar et al., 2014). The family stress model has been generally supported by research across several cultures and countries (Zietz et al., 2022).

However, associating all lower-income families with poor parenting and higher-income families with good parenting is an inaccurate stereotype (Luthar & Latendresse, 2005). Children from higher-income backgrounds may also experience mental health problems, such as heightened anxiety, compared to children from lower-income families (Luthar & Latendresse, 2005). This increased anxiety may be due to a lack of quality family time as a result of greater extracurricular commitments for children and parental career obligations (Luthar, 2003). Parents in more affluent families can also exert high pressure to achieve academically, increasing stress and anxiety in children (Luthar & Becker, 2002). It is important to consider potential stressors in families across the socioeconomic spectrum.

2.1.2 Stress Spillover and Contagion

In the family stress model, stressors encountered by family members can impact the child through *spillover effects* or processes of *stress contagion* (Sears et al., 2016; Waters et al., 2014). That is, if a parent is experiencing financial stress, this stress can *spill over* into other domains, such as their parenting behaviors and interactions with their child (Liu & Doan, 2020; Sears et al., 2016). A related process, which occurs more directly between dyad members, is *stress contagion*, mirroring a social partner's emotions and physiology. For example, Waters et al. (2014) found that infants exhibited higher heart rate activity when interacting with their mother after their mother was exposed to a negative social stressor in a separate room, compared to infants whose mothers did not encounter a negative social stressor. Furthermore, mothers who experienced the negative stressor and their infants showed greater physiological covariation over time, such that mothers with higher physiological activation had infants with higher heart rate responses. This suggests that stress responses are socially regulated, and mothers' and infants' stress systems can influence each other (Waters et al., 2014).

As children and their caregivers interact, during stressful or non-stressful circumstances, their stress physiology and behavior may become aligned during their interactions. In fact, contingent social interactions with coordinated responses between parents and their young children are crucial in supporting children's development of self-regulation and later school adjustment (Harrist et al., 1994; Lobo & Lunkenheimer, 2020). A key ingredient that underlies these successful reciprocal interactions is *synchrony*, which involves the dynamic coupling and coordination of behaviors or physiology between two partners in real time (Bell, 2020; Feldman, 2007). Stress research has evidenced synchrony, or attunement, of mother–child cortisol levels in infancy and toddlerhood (Hibel et al., 2015), and how this attunement may change during acute stress. This attunement, important for the development of a child's regulatory capabilities (Lobo & Lunkenheimer, 2020), decreased during a stress task (Hibel et al., 2015).

Children who have experienced higher levels of family adversity may show lower levels of behavioral and neural synchrony with their parents (Hoyniak et al., 2021). Furthermore, for children from families experiencing economic hardship or with histories of maltreatment, synchrony may not be associated with greater interaction quality (DePasquale, 2020) and may play a role in the transmission of stress between family members. Parents who suffer from depression may engage in more negative parenting behaviors or display more negative affect, potentially impacting child cortisol levels (Apter-Levi et al., 2016). Thus, it is not always optimal to be in a state of synchrony with a caregiver. It may be important for children and parents to shift flexibly in and out of synchrony with each other, particularly during states of negative emotionality.

2.1.3 Parenting Styles and Setting Limits

Young children can be reared with several parenting styles, which can be described along dimensions of warmth and control (Baumrind, 1971). The *authoritative* parenting style, high in both warmth and control, which provides both nurturance and firm limits to children, has been linked to positive child outcomes (Baumrind, 1971). In contrast, an *authoritarian* parenting style is characterized by high levels of control (i.e., setting strict limits) but is low in warmth. Finally, the *permissive* parenting style is high in warmth, but does not enforce limits or attempt to control children's behavior. Authoritative parenting, high in both warmth and limit setting, has been linked to the most positive outcomes for children in European American families, although other parenting styles may promote positive outcomes in other cultural groups (Bornstein, 2012).

Parenting styles and behaviors have been linked to children's stress physiology. Fathers' authoritarian parenting, specifically fathers' physical coercion, is associated with increased child hair cortisol levels (Isaac et al., 2023). Children who experienced more maternal control or criticism during a challenge task showed lower parasympathetic nervous system activity (Skowron et al., 2011). Children of mothers with anxiety, who displayed instances of overcontrol (e.g., a parent's excessive regulation of their child's behavior), showed greater reactivity to a challenge task (Borelli et al., 2018). Furthermore, parents' poor monitoring and supervision, indicative of a permissive parenting style, is associated with higher immune activation and inflammation in children, biological processes that may lead to poor later health (Byrne et al., 2017; Miller et al., 2011). Low parental monitoring has also been linked to children having flatter diurnal cortisol slopes, indicating HPA axis dysregulation (Martin et al., 2014). Thus, both authoritarian and permissive parenting styles have been linked to less desirable indices of child stress physiology and responses to challenge.

2.1.4 Parental Discipline

In addition to parenting styles, examined along dimensions of warmth and control, parental discipline use is also linked to child outcomes. Power-assertive discipline is a type of parental discipline that demands obedience and includes the use of corporal punishment (e.g., spanking) and has been linked to child internalizing and externalizing symptoms over time (Sturge-Apple et al., 2022). Corporal punishment in and of itself has been shown to have a negative effect on children, including lower cognitive performance (Ferguson, 2013).

Research on family dynamics and later child behavioral problems has stemmed from work by Patterson and colleagues on *coercion theory* (Patterson, 2002; Smith et al., 2014). Coercive family dynamics involve a cycle of behaviors where a caregiver's behavior unintentionally reinforces a child's difficult behavior. This happens when caregivers respond to a child's difficult behavior with anger, hostility, or harsh discipline, signaling that angry outbursts are acceptable ways to behave, or, in contrast, by the parent withdrawing and giving in to their child. In the short term, the child may comply and stop the difficult behavior. However, over time, the child may learn that opposition or defiance is a helpful way to meet their needs (Smith et al., 2014). This cycle may reinforce parents' dependence on harsh disciplinary responses and continue inconsistent discipline and difficult child behavior (Hakman et al., 2009; Martin et al., 2014; Patterson, 1982). Promoting positive parenting behaviors, such as effective and calm limit setting, may reduce these negative cycles (Smith et al., 2014). Continued coercive dynamics in the family may put children at risk of developing antisocial behavior (Granic & Patterson, 2006;

Smith et al., 2014), compromising additional developmental outcomes such as academic success and emotion regulation (Granic & Patterson, 2006).

2.1.5 Lack of Warmth and Exposure to Harsh Parenting

Family environments with a lack of parental warmth or exposure to harsh parenting may also be stressful for children. Parental warmth involves affection and acceptance toward the child and is a positively regarded dimension of parenting (Deater-Deckard et al., 2011). Conversely, harsh parenting, including over-reactivity, hostility, and physical punishment, predicts negative outcomes for children, such as child behavior problems (Lunkenheimer et al., 2017; MacKenzie et al., 2015). In dyads of children and mothers with higher levels of harsh parenting, dyadic coregulation may be impacted, as mothers were less likely to couple their parenting behaviors with their child's behavior (Lunkenheimer et al., 2017). In these dyads, children are also less likely to benefit from their mother's parenting practices that support child autonomy (Lunkenheimer et al., 2017).

Early harsh parenting can exacerbate the effects of stress on cortisol reactivity in children (Jaffee et al., 2015). Children's cortisol reactivity to a stressor differs depending on whether they experience harsh and nonresponsive parenting early in childhood coupled with concurrent exposure to traumatic events at age 10. Participants who had experienced traumatic events in middle childhood and experienced higher levels of harsh parenting in early childhood showed the lowest levels of cortisol reactivity, illustrating a blunted cortisol profile (Jaffee et al., 2015). Children of mothers who reported more yelling and shouting, indicating harsh parenting, showed higher cortisol levels when interacting with adult strangers (Hastings et al., 2011). Thus, exposure to harsh parenting appears to promote cortisol reactivity in children. Furthermore, children with dismissing attachment (a type of insecure attachment where caregivers may be unresponsive to their needs) show higher stress reactivity (SNS activity) during a help-seeking vignette (Borelli et al., 2023).

Stress in parent-child relationships can range from isolated experiences of harshness or conflict, which likely trigger only an acute stress response, to more prolonged and traumatic instances of child maltreatment, which entail chronic stress. Experiences of maltreatment can trigger a cascade of disruptions in developmental processes (Cicchetti, 2013). Furthermore, children who experience maltreatment are likely to experience other disruptions to daily life and stressors related to family relationships, such as being placed in foster care (Dozier et al., 2009). Maltreatment is a potent stressor when experienced at any age (Cicchetti, 2013; Cicchetti & Toth, 2005).

2.1.6 Unpredictability and Lack of Family Routines May Tune Child Stress Physiology

How families organize their schedules, day-to-day activities, and routines can increase or reduce stress in children's lives. Predictability is a feature of the home and family environment that shapes children's experiences and their developing stress-response systems (Davis & Glynn, 2024; Smith & Pollak, 2020; Ugarte & Hastings, 2024). The predictability of parent signals (for example, sensory inputs or parent mood) is an important part of the biological, social, and environmental processes that shape children's brain development (Davis & Glynn, 2024). A lack of stable family routines can increase a child's exposure to unpredictability, thereby increasing stress. When signals from the environment are unpredictable, children are at greater risk of increased anxiety and depressive symptoms, negative affectivity, and poorer cognitive development, including decreased effortful control (Davis & Glynn, 2024).

Some home environments are characterized by high levels of unpredictability, disorganization, or unstable family routines, which can be described as household chaos, usually measured using the Confusion, Hubbub, and Order Scale (CHAOS; Matheny et al., 1995). In home environments with higher levels of chaos, parent responsiveness may be lower, affecting child executive functions and regulatory capabilities (Andrews et al., 2021). Household chaos during the preschool years is associated with higher cortisol reactivity in middle childhood (Doom et al., 2018). An early environment with greater levels of chaos in preschool may heighten reactivity to stressors, as a way of preparing children's stress biology for a future environment with household chaos in middle childhood (Doom et al., 2018).

Stressors that occur in the family environment may result in major changes to family routines. For example, divorce is a change to the family environment and a common stressor that involves a major change in routines. Children of divorced families may be at risk of experiencing a variety of stressors, although positive and high-quality parenting following divorce is protective for child outcomes (Vélez et al., 2011). Other normative stressors that occur in children's lives, such as the addition of a new sibling, increases in arguments between or with parents, and changes in parental finances, result in changes to children's daily routines (Davis & Glynn, 2024).

During the COVID-19 pandemic, families with more consistent routines, such as children going to bed at the same time each night, had lower rates of child depressive symptoms and conduct problems (Glynn et al., 2021). The protective effects of routines persisted after accounting for important household characteristics such as income, food insecurity, and maternal psychological distress. In another sample, families who followed more routines during the pandemic were buffered from the negative effects of COVID-19 stress on family resilience (Bates et al., 2021). It appears that a predictable and consistent family environment is protective for children, even in stressful circumstances.

2.1.7 Parent–Child Conflict

The parent–child relationship changes as children develop. Infants depend on their caregivers to meet their needs and require support, supervision, and help with emotion regulation. Thus, stressors during this period may involve inconsistent caregiver support or being separated from a parent (Gunnar et al., 2009). Toddlers gain greater autonomy and may frequently use the word "no," hit, or say "I don't want to," which can lead to potential conflicts between parents and young children. As children develop, their need for autonomy also increases, and parent–child conflict may arise as children negotiate for increased autonomy.

Parents serve multiple functions in their children's lives. The parent–child relationship has been regarded as being made up of several domains or goals (Grusec, 2011): protection, mutual reciprocity (responding to each other), control/discipline, guided learning, and modeling appropriate behaviors (Grusec, 2011). These domains require parents to use different parenting strategies and behaviors at different times and respond to their child's needs (Grusec, 2011). It can be difficult for parents to navigate between different parenting goals, especially in challenging situations. When faced with a stressful situation or a child's distress, maintaining a balance between warmth and limit-setting may become difficult. This circumstance may result in harsh parenting practices during parent–child conflict.

Some parent–child conflicts are inevitable and normative. However, conflicts that are repeated, prolonged, or have no productive resolution may be a source of stress for children and parents alike. A daily diary study examined parent–child conflict reported by youth ages 8 to 13 for 8 weeks in connection with child diurnal cortisol levels (Kuhlman et al., 2016). Increasing levels of parent–child conflict were associated with several indices of HPA functioning, including increased total cortisol output and changes in diurnal rhythms, such as a flatter diurnal slope of cortisol and higher cortisol levels at bedtime (Kuhlman et al., 2016). *Risky families*, a term proposed by Repetti and colleagues (2002), has been used to describe families or family environments that are characterized by high family conflict, anger or aggression, and limited or no warmth. Children growing up in risky family environments who experience frequent conflict in the family or between parents may show an upregulated stress response (Gunnar et al., 2015; Repetti et al., 2002). Importantly, child characteristics may moderate the association between interparental conflict and child outcomes. For example, children with an irritable temperament may experience poorer outcomes in the context of high conflict between parents (Hentges et al., 2015).

2.2 Familial Sources of Resilience

Developmental research has highlighted many pathways linking stressors that occur in the family system to child stress, but these same pathways may also reveal potential strategies to promote resilience in children and their families. Some of the primary ways to support resilience through the family include social buffering, promoting sensitive parenting, emotion socialization, stress reduction for parents, and predictable family routines.

2.2.1 Attachment Figures as Social Buffers Against Stress

The attachment relationship emerges early between infants and their caregivers (Bowlby, 1969; Siegel, 2001). Infants seek proximity to their attachment figure, who serves as a secure base during threatening or stressful situations.

The presence and availability of an attachment figure can buffer or reduce the activity of stress-response systems like the HPA axis (Hostinar et al., 2014). This protective effect may be especially important for children who are temperamentally fearful or inhibited (Nachmias et al., 1996).

Parents and attachment figures regulate children's responses to stressful events and challenges (Hostinar et al., 2014). However, each parent-child relationship is different, and there may be differences in how parents buffer their children from stress. In one study, parents helped their children prepare for a laboratory-based public speaking task. Children were randomly assigned to either have their parents help them prepare for the speech or prepare alone. A control group of children did not complete the stressful task (Parenteau et al., 2020). In this study, parents did not buffer their children's cortisol reactivity on average, which differs from previous studies that demonstrate parental social buffering in this same age group (Hostinar et al., 2015a, 2015b). This study found an interaction effect of condition and parental education level. Children whose parents had less than a four-year college degree showed a buffered profile, with lower cortisol levels when they received parental support, and children whose parents had a four-year college degree exhibited higher cortisol reactivity with parental support compared to children in the alone or control groups (Parenteau et al., 2020). It is possible that parents with higher education provided a different type of support to their child when preparing for the stressor, such as emphasizing the child's performance, thereby increasing their cortisol levels (Parenteau et al., 2020). This study exemplifies differences between parents in their ability to buffer children's stress due to different factors, such as parental education or the type of support provided to their child.

In summary, social support is a powerful tool to promote children's resilience (Miller et al., 2011; Miller & Chen, 2013). However, early-life stress exposure, attachment security, temperament, and pubertal development may impact the developing stress system and the effectiveness of social buffering (Gunnar et al., 2019; Hostinar et al., 2015a; Nachmias et al., 1996). Questions remain about the specific factors that might influence parents' ability to buffer child stress responses, which is vital in advancing our understanding of how to promote these processes to foster child resilience.

2.2.2 Supporting Sensitive Parenting

Parenting that is supportive, sensitive, and nurturing can buffer children from stress and protect against the deleterious effects of early childhood socioeconomic deprivation on health (Miller & Chen, 2013). Supportive family relationships also promote resilience among children who have experienced maltreatment (Afifi & MacMillan, 2011). The beneficial causal effects of family support are also well-supported by intervention studies demonstrating that improvements in parenting can shift child biological outcomes. For example, the Attachment and Biobehavioral Catch-up (ABC) program promotes contingent and sensitive parental responding and has been shown to normalize children's diurnal cortisol activity compared to the atypical patterns seen in children exposed to adversity (Dozier et al., 2006). The ABC program targets nurturance and synchrony in parent-child interactions (Bernard et al., 2013). In addition, 9-year-old children whose parents had received ABC in infancy showed positive impacts on their autonomic regulation, illustrated by higher respiratory sinus arrhythmia and lower heart rate during a parent-child interaction (Tabachnick et al., 2019). The Filming Interactions to Nurture Development (FIND) is another parent coaching intervention, which is focused on promoting contingent *serve-and-return* interactions and has been shown to reduce psychopathology symptoms in children with high cortisol values (i.e., high area under the curve) in response to a stressor (Liu et al., 2021). Serve and return interactions are those where children "serve" invitations to their caregivers by reaching out via their actions, vocalizations, or gaze, and caregivers "return" the child's serve by responding with contingent behavior (Liu et al., 2021; Shonkoff & Bales, 2011). Several intervention programs that impact child resilience to stress through targeting sensitive parenting and secure attachment relationships are described in Section 7.

2.2.3 Parental Socialization of Emotion and Emotion Regulation

Children first learn about emotions and strategies for regulating and expressing them from their parents, a process termed parental socialization of emotion (Eisenberg et al., 1998; England-Mason & Gonzalez, 2020; Morris et al., 2017). These processes include parents modeling appropriate emotion regulation for their children, various parenting practices (such as emotion coaching), and the impact of the emotional climate of the family on the child (England-Mason & Gonzalez, 2020; Morris et al., 2017). Parents' emotional socialization behaviors and emotion-related parenting practices impact children's understanding of emotions and their ability to regulate their emotions (Eisenberg, 2020). In addition, parents' own emotion regulation is an important predictor of child emotion regulation, both directly and indirectly (Morris et al., 2017).

Supportive early caregiving behaviors also shape children's future reactivity to stressors and how they regulate their emotions throughout childhood. By providing sensitive and responsive caregiving, where infants engage in mutual, contingent, and reciprocal interactions with their caregivers, parents can promote children's capability for mutual regulation of emotion (Cole et al., 2004; Lobo & Lunkenheimer, 2020).

Notably, children who experience early-life stress may exhibit altered development of these capabilities (Blair, 2010). Furthermore, for children exposed to adversity, navigating a complex array of emotional demands and stressors in the caregiving relationship means that adaptive emotion regulation may look different, as some strategies considered "optimal" for other children may confer risk (Thompson & Calkins, 1996). For children exposed to adversity, maternal emotional socialization behaviors may play a role in regulating child physiological functioning (Buhler-Wassman et al., 2021). In a sample of families primarily recruited through the Department of Child Services, mothers who were more disengaged from socializing their child's emotions had children with higher cortisol levels and flatter diurnal slopes compared to children of mothers with engaged and supportive emotion socialization profiles (Buhler-Wassmann et al., 2021). Thus, parent socialization of emotion is an important process for promoting resilience among children exposed to stress.

2.2.4 Stress Reduction for Parents

Reducing parents' stress levels is a promising solution to boost family resilience and improve child outcomes. Programs that help parents manage stress levels and teach parents tools to cope with stress, such as mindfulness, have positive effects for their children. For instance, parent participation in a mindfulness-based stress reduction program resulted in beneficial effects for their children with developmental delays, particularly in child measures of self-control and teacher-reported social skill improvements (Lewallen & Neece, 2015). This study illustrates that stress reduction for parents is important for boosting positive child outcomes.

Parent mental health treatment and programs that support parents' self-regulation and executive function skills ultimately benefit child stress levels (see Section 7). Parent mental health and child mental health are strongly intertwined (Bennett et al., 2012). Parents who can buffer children from stress typically have adequate mental health and established executive function and regulatory abilities, allowing parents to promote these abilities in their children (Shonkoff & Fisher, 2013). Promoting parent self-regulation may be important to prevent spillover effects of stress on children (Sears et al., 2016). Importantly, these regulatory capabilities are unlikely to develop in parents via the simple provision of information and support; rather, they appear to require more intensive coaching or parent training programs (Shonkoff & Fisher, 2013).

2.2.5 Predictable Routines as a Source of Resilience

A predictable and stable home environment has been consistently linked to children's resilience and adaptive coping. To promote positive child development and healthy development of stress systems, predictable family routines have a strong protective effect (Davis & Glynn, 2024; Glynn et al., 2021). The presence of predictable family routines can buffer children from stressors. As described, children from families following more routines during the COVID-19 pandemic had lower rates of depressive symptoms and conduct problems (Glynn et al., 2021). Parents who maintained stable routines during the pandemic were able to buffer the effects of pandemic-related stress on children's clinical symptomatology (Cohodes et al., 2021). Multiple pre-pandemic studies also illustrate the positive impact of parental structuring of the child environment and highlight the beneficial effects of stability and predictability (Davis & Glynn, 2024). Consistency in family routines may buffer the effect of exposure to early adversity on later outcomes (Koss et al., 2020). When considering how to promote child resilience to stress within family systems, effective strategies include supporting parents and caregivers by alleviating stress, fostering sensitive caregiving, and providing resources to establish predictable family routines.

3 Stress and Belonging in Peer Relationships

As children develop and enter a broader social environment beyond their families, the influence of peers intensifies. Early experiences can shape how children's stress-response systems react in social interactions. For instance, children experiencing maltreatment (i.e., abuse or neglect) have been shown to have a blunted cortisol response to a social stress task and also report a smaller group of perceived friends when compared to age-matched, non-maltreated children (Negriff et al., 2020). Adverse social experiences may not only change children's stress responses, but also their perceptions of social support and interactions.

Peer relationships become increasingly important for helping children cope with stress across development (Adams et al., 2011). Having a friend present during a negative social event buffers against stress reactivity. For example, 5th and 6th graders (averaging 10.3 years old) from the greater Montreal metropolitan area who had a best friend present during negative events showed fewer increases in HPA axis activity and less change in global self-worth across the negative events (Adams et al., 2011) compared to situations when a best friend was not present. This finding illustrates how peer relationships buffer stress responses in early childhood and may protect self-esteem. However, peers can also be a source of stress and social rejection. This Section examines the challenges and benefits of reliance on peer support.

3.1 Peer-related Sources of Stress

3.1.1 Peer Victimization and Bullying in Childhood

Peer victimization and bullying remain concerningly prevalent among school-aged children (Olweus & Limber, 2010), with consequences for children's educational, social, and mental health outcomes. Peer victimization can be defined as "being the target, directly or indirectly, of an aggressive action" (Adams et al., 2020, p. 1). While sometimes used synonymously with bullying, peer victimization is different, as bullying implies there is a power imbalance between the aggressor and the victim (Adams et al., 2020). Bullying has been commonly described as behaviors by one or more people that are repeated, intentional, and negative (unpleasant or hurtful), which are directed against a person who has difficulty defending himself or herself (Olweus & Limber, 2010). Children appearing as "different" compared to most others tend to be at greater risk of being victimized (Armitage, 2021). Bullying based on race, ethnicity, religion, gender, or sexual orientation has been described with more specific phrases such as *bias-based bullying* (Walton, 2018).

Early experiences of peer victimization have long-term consequences for child development. For example, one study found that children with high levels of cumulative peer victimization experiences in second grade (average age 8 years old) show suppressed effortful control by sixth grade (Troop-Gordon et al., 2017). A systematic review of studies conducted with children as young as 5 years old revealed that one of the most consistent findings was a blunted cortisol response during stressful tasks among victimized youth (Kliewer et al., 2019). Not many studies collect biological stress response measures (e.g., cortisol, inflammatory markers) to examine associations between peer victimization and health in young children (Kliewer et al., 2019), making it difficult to understand how later health and stress response patterns are impacted by peer relationships in early childhood.

Furthermore, bullying is a frequently reported stressor for children (Vanaelst et al., 2012) with serious adverse mental, health, and financial costs to families and the broader society (Wolke & Lereya, 2015). While bullying rates seemed to decline during the home quarantine period of the COVID-19 pandemic (Vaillancourt et al., 2021), children from diverse and marginalized backgrounds were disproportionately affected by other pandemic-related stressors (Jost et al., 2023).

Additionally, the repercussions of bullying extend well beyond childhood, as evidenced by a 50-year longitudinal study of a cohort born in 1958 in the United Kingdom. Individuals whose parents reported their exposure to childhood bullying at ages 7 and 11 experienced heightened distress at ages 23 and 50 (Takizawa et al., 2014). Furthermore, children who had experienced frequent bullying were also more likely to experience difficulties in social, health, and economic domains in adulthood. Another longitudinal study showed that adults who retrospectively reported being bullied in childhood showed larger increases in C-reactive protein (CRP) levels in adulthood, an indicator of low-grade systemic inflammation that predicts heightened risk of cardiovascular disease, compared to those who were not bullied (Copeland et al., 2014).

Bullying occurring online, also known as cyberbullying, involves intimidating, taunting, harassing, and threatening behaviors that take place via an online medium (Shetgiri, 2013). One in 5 children ages 9 to 12 from the United States reported being cyberbullied, a perpetrator of cyberbullying, or having seen cyberbullying occur (Hinduja & Patchin, 2023). However, the prevalence of stress from cyberbullying may be more difficult to identify among children under the age of 10, as not much research focuses on how younger children access and engage with online platforms compared to adolescents.

3.1.2 Social Withdrawal

Children tend to form friendships with the peers they meet regularly, a phenomenon known as "propinquity" (Hartup & Abecassis, 2002). Specifically, children tend to become friends with other children with whom they share similarities (Hartup, 1996; Liberman & Shaw, 2019). These shared attributes can be related to gender, age, racial and ethnic background, proximity,

SES, and shared interests (Hartup & Abecassis, 2002; Liberman & Shaw, 2019). Children who are different from others along one or more attributes or who suffer from social anxiety may struggle to form friendships and could fall prey to social withdrawal and loneliness. For instance, one US study showed that African American and Latino middle school students felt lonelier if their classrooms had lower levels of ethnic diversity (Juvonen et al., 2006), possibly due to having fewer opportunities to form friendships with children from the same cultural background.

Multiple theories and measures have been proposed to study social withdrawal. Yet, most approaches similarly capture social withdrawal as a behavioral pattern characterized by various forms of solitude (Rubin & Coplan, 2004). Specifically, children who are socially withdrawn consistently withdraw from friends across time and context (Rubin et al., 2013). Some socially withdrawn children experience difficulty with having a large number of friends (Pedersen et al., 2007), but others may not. However, regardless of the number of friends they may have, socially withdrawn children often befriend children who share similar psychosocial difficulties (Rubin et al., 2009). For example, a study involving a sample of 2,437 American children with an average age of 10 found that, although socially withdrawn youth and their non-socially withdrawn counterparts were equally likely to report having stable, lasting friendships, the socially withdrawn children often formed friendships with peers who were similarly withdrawn and victimized (Ladd et al., 2011). Therefore, they were more likely to spend more time in solitude, which may ultimately lead to maladjustment.

Moreover, social withdrawal and anxiety in early childhood have been associated with peer rejection and low popularity, suggesting bidirectional associations between social anxiety and peer difficulties (Rubin et al., 2009). Peer acceptance and rejection have been linked to changes in cortisol levels (Behnsen et al., 2018; Gunnar et al., 2003). Preschool-aged children who have been rejected by their peers show higher cortisol levels compared to non-rejected children (Gunnar et al., 2003). Furthermore, 9-year-old children from the Netherlands who had experienced peer exclusion had higher cortisol levels at school (Peters et al., 2011). This effect was less pronounced for children with more friends or better-quality friendships. These findings underscore the importance of peer relationships for navigating daily social challenges to prevent early maladaptive activation of the stress response (Negriff et al., 2020).

3.2 Peers and Friends as Sources of Resilience

High-quality relationships with peers are so integral to resilience that some researchers have considered peer acceptance as a facet of resilience (Bolger &

Patterson, 2003). Indeed, research studies with children who experienced maltreatment have shown that having a close friendship can predict better mental health (Cicchetti, 2013). These findings emphasize the importance of close friendships for buffering against negative stress-related outcomes.

3.2.1 Social Support Promotes Resilience

Research has also documented the protective role of social support from friends and family against the "double burden" of negative peer interactions and large-scale stressors such as the COVID-19 pandemic, as shown in a study of children ages 9 to 16 years old from Norway (Thorvaldsen et al., 2024). Most children who had been victimized by bullying or harassment were resilient (77 percent as measured by the Strengths and Difficulties Questionnaire), often with the help of their social support network. Specifically, bullied children reported having friends as a protective factor, amongst other factors such as familial support, emotional and physical well-being, and positive self-esteem (Thorvaldsen et al., 2024).

Because resilience is a complex developmental process that is influenced by various factors throughout development (Cicchetti & Blender, 2006), interventions aimed at promoting healthy peer interactions in each developmental period could offer a promising avenue for reducing the prevalence and the impact of bullying and peer victimization. Concrete actions could be implemented to prevent bullying and peer victimization in childhood, in turn decreasing its potential stress-related effects. Interventions fostering strong social support networks with parental and peer support can help to mitigate the effects of bullying (Armitage, 2021).

3.2.2 The Broader Social Support Network

In light of these findings, interventions leveraging the influential factors in the broader social environment may provide additional benefits. For example, primary care practitioners, child psychologists, and social workers serve as critical gateways to screen for stress-related outcomes in children to assess for potential impacts such as depression, anxiety, and other mental health problems (Shetgiri, 2013). They can also provide families with support and resources for further evaluation.

Further, schools play a crucial role in encouraging positive peer relationships, therefore serving as key stakeholders in implementing more effective anti-bullying campaigns and interventions. A meta-analysis with youth ages 4 to 17 years old found that anti-bullying interventions are not only effective at reducing rates of bullying, but they can also alleviate youth mental health difficulties (Fraguas et al., 2021). Furthermore, at the institutional level, evidence-based training and resources are needed to educate children and families about the benefits of positive peer relationships. This strategy could help prevent stress overload from adverse social experiences such as victimization or bullying. Such education and resources could help children become better equipped to cope as they navigate challenging social interactions.

Interventions targeting shyness and social anxiety may also promote social skill development and healthy peer interactions (Hang et al., 2024). For instance, Rubin and Chronis-Tuscano (2021) developed an early intervention program aimed at preschoolers called the Turtle Program, a multimodal intervention teaching socioemotional skills to 3- to 5-year-olds who were identified as extremely shy or inhibited. Ongoing work in this program will allow measures of children's emotional reactivity and autonomic functioning, along with other goals of managing children's anxiety symptoms, further identifying how children's stress response measures are impacted by peer relationship dynamics.

Parents, educators, and practitioners can also educate children about power dynamics within peer relationships (Zhu, 2023). When possible, integrating these resources with technology such as wearable devices and monitoring apps that track stress physiology may empower children to recognize signs of stress and engage their coping strategies (Masten & Barnes, 2018).

4 Stress and the School Environment

"I don't want to go to school." Seven words that most parents and guardians hear at some point in their child's school career. Starting around 5 years old, most children spend the majority of their waking hours at school in a typical week. While going to school entails meeting new friends, learning, and developing new skills, transitioning to school and the daily school experience are not without challenges (Harrison & Murray, 2015; Jiang et al., 2021). As an adaptive response to a real or interpreted threat of these challenges, stress will likely emerge in some way and at some point for all young students in their school careers and can be positive, tolerable, or toxic. Life events and stressors experienced outside the school context can also greatly impact children's adjustment and achievement in school (Jimenez et al., 2016; Masten et al., 1988). This section explores the various sources of stress in schools for children, the indicators of stress observed in schools, and school-based solutions to promote student well-being and resilience.

4.1 Sources of School-based Stress

Out-of-home care can elicit a stress response in children as young as 2 years old, with greater biological stress reactivity during daycare days compared to weekends (Dettling et al., 1999; Tout et al., 1998; Vermeer & van IJzendoorn, 2006). As they enter formal schooling, children may find various aspects of their school experience stressful. Stressors can range in severity from daily hassles, such as fatigue and frustration while learning new information (Sotardi, 2016), to more acute stressors such as daily separation from caregivers to severe incidents like threats to physical safety at school, including school shootings and peer violence. Notably, the stress that children experience through life events that occur outside of the school context is also carried with them when they enter the school building. This section focuses on sources of stress at school while acknowledging that the effects of these stressors can be catalyzed and compounded by children's individual characteristics and cumulative life experiences.

4.1.1 Transitioning to School

Whether it is a child's very first day of school or merely the start of a new school year, transitions to school can introduce many uncertainties, new fears, and be riddled with the challenges of adjusting to new routines and novel social environments. Starting school is undoubtedly stressful. Even though this is a normative transition and expected change in most children's lives, it is a significant change, nonetheless. Moreover, the transition into formal schooling marks a crucial developmental shift in what is expected of children regarding their behavior, attention, and goals, as well as their social interactions with others (Rimm-Kaufman & Pianta, 2000), which can introduce myriad stressors to a child's life.

School transitions can induce a stress response in children as young as 4 years old (Groeneveld et al., 2013). Children's cortisol levels tend to increase during the transition from preschool to formal schooling (Parent et al., 2019), but average cortisol levels tend to decrease and stabilize as the school year progresses and children adapt to the experience (Hall & Lindorff, 2017; Turner-Cobb et al., 2008). However, evidence for cortisol recovery after the initial start of school is mixed, with many other studies reporting no evidence of significant decreases in cortisol as the school year progressed (Groeneveld et al., 2013; Gutteling et al., 2005; Russ et al., 2012). Taken together, this literature highlights how stress-response systems produce additional cortisol during school days, potentially to help children adapt to the increased demands of school. These findings also suggest that there is likely a prolonged period of adaptation to the school experience for children during their first year of school.

School transitions can also bring about environmental changes that introduce new stressors or exacerbate existing stressors. For example, the transition from elementary school to middle school can negatively impact school belonging and teacher affiliation and, in some cases, is associated with increases in experiences of bullying (Espelage et al., 2015). Transitions in general are ripe with novelty, which ultimately encourages adaptation, yet the initial disruption to children's expected environment is likely to be stressful for many reasons. Supporting children in times of change can include normalizing emotional reactions to the discomfort of change, helping them to recognize and establish new routines, and reinforcing positive outcomes associated with the change.

4.1.2 The Classroom Environment

Terms like school and classroom "climate" have been broadly used to describe many facets of the educational environment that are linked to student outcomes and psychosocial well-being (Freiberg, 2005). Supportive classroom climates are instrumental in nurturing child development, whereas stress-laden classrooms can undermine student success and well-being (Marzano & Marzano, 2003). For example, classroom chaos, characterized by a high level of noise, lack of regular routines, unpredictability, overcrowding, and unclear expectations, can be an impactful source of stress for young learners (Maxwell, 2010). Young children's reactions to these environmental discomforts can further disrupt the classroom climate, possibly resulting in disciplinary responses from teachers. Cultural mismatch between children and educators can exacerbate student stress and is evidenced to underlie stress-related health disparities in adolescence and young adulthood (Chen et al., 2023). Educators can reduce stress by cultivating a classroom environment with minimal distractions (Fisher et al., 2014) and establishing clear and equitable expectations of student behavior in the class community. Crucially, equitable treatment of students in educational contexts demands that educators are aware of their own cultural biases and how their background informs their pedagogy.

Educators' own well-being also defines the classroom climate. High stress and burnout can impede educators' capacity to provide a nurturing and constructive classroom environment (Zinsser et al., 2013) and can result in greater teacher-student conflict or negative responses to children's behavior (Buettner et al., 2016; Whitaker et al., 2015). Teachers' stress levels predict preschool children's behavioral functioning (Jeon et al., 2019) and declines in elementary school children's school adjustment and success (Arens & Morin, 2016; Herman et al., 2018). Furthermore, higher teacher burnout predicts higher cortisol awakening responses in elementary school children, thus emphasizing how stress contagion in the classroom can have ramifications for children's physiological stress response (Oberle & Schonert-Reichl, 2016). A vicious cycle can emerge whereby teacher stress can exacerbate student stress, leading to more negative student behavioral responses and emotional disturbances that further augment educator stress (Jennings & Greenberg, 2009). Therefore, reducing the environmental sources of stress embedded within a classroom context and mitigating educator stress are critical for cultivating classroom communities that promote student well-being and reduce school-based stress for all.

4.1.3 Relationships at School

For most children, relationships with teachers are some of the first influential relationships they form with adults outside their family unit. The student-teacher relationship is a formative developmental experience that can be both a source of stress and a powerful resource as students adjust to school (Hamre & Pianta, 2001). When asked to report their source of stress in school, children described teacher interactions as a major stressor, particularly when teachers reprimand children and show favoritism (Agrawal et al., 2010). Academic expectations, particularly as children advance in their education, also introduce stress when children perceive themselves as unable to perform as expected or desired (Sotardi, 2016) or when they fear disappointing teachers and parents (Wong, 2015). Conflict in student-teacher relationships has also been associated with impairments in the biological stress regulatory processes in elementary students (Ahnert et al., 2012) and spikes in cortisol levels during child-teacher interactions in children as young as four years old (Lisonbee et al., 2008).

Stressors in the student-teacher relationship can accentuate maladjustment, but having a high-quality relationship with a teacher can be protective against the consequences of stress (Ladd & Burgess, 2001). For example, Elledge et al. (2016) found that children who had above-average quality relationships with teachers were less likely to report experiencing peer victimization despite being rejected by peers compared to counterparts with lower-quality relationships with teachers. Ultimately, when children feel supported and encouraged by their teachers, they are less likely to experience stress at school and more likely to exhibit diurnal cortisol profiles indicative of adaptive stress regulation (Ahnert et al., 2012). Thus, student-teacher relationships can impact young children's lives by magnifying or mitigating stress at school.

Adults at school are not the only sources of stress and support for young children. Upon entering formal schooling, children are inducted into a community of people who define their educational experience, most of whom are their peers. As described in detail in Section 3, peer relationships can be uniquely stressful as children seek peer acceptance and learn to navigate the idiosyncrasies of forming friendships (Rubin et al., 2011). Children may encounter many peer-related stressors at school, such as trying to learn alongside disruptive classmates, friendship challenges, peer exclusion, and bullying or victimization. Peer rejection at school is associated with both overactivated and dysregulated biological stress reactivity (Peters et al., 2011).

Crucially, there may be bidirectional associations between children's stress reactivity and the quality of their engagement with peers at school. Early childhood adversity can lead to dysregulation of the stress response system (Gunnar, 2000), which can in turn lead to socioemotional difficulties (Thompson, 2014). For example, children with higher cortisol levels show greater social wariness and behavioral inhibition in kindergarten (Smider et al., 2002), and greater cortisol reactivity in response to a social stressor task has been linked to social difficulties in school (Mathewson et al., 2012). Lower peer acceptance and greater peer rejection have been associated with higher cortisol levels (Behnsen et al., 2018; Gunnar et al., 2003) as described in Section 3. Conversely, children with supportive peer relationships are more likely to demonstrate greater academic engagement and overall school adjustment (Perdue et al., 2009; Wentzel et al., 2009). Taken together, these findings suggest that alterations in stress-response systems can be both an outcome of stressful peer interactions and a predictor of future social withdrawal or peer difficulties, suggesting the importance of intervening to interrupt these vicious cycles.

4.2 Recognizing School-based Stress

4.2.1 Identifying Signs of Stress in the Classroom

Recognizing the manifestation of stress in children at school is critical for knowing how to address it, support the distressed child, and prevent further stress-related consequences. Children under the age of 10 who are stressed often react overtly with behaviors like crying, aggressive outbursts, emotional swings, and anxious behaviors like nail biting, hair twirling, or obsessive worry about routines and "what comes next" (Jewett & Peterson, 2002). As discussed previously, young children may also express physical complaints in response to stress like headaches and stomachaches, and more frequent requests to use the bathroom (Jewett & Peterson, 2002). Meanwhile, some children are more prone to internalizing reactions to stress, appearing socially withdrawn, detached, or distracted in class (Zahn-Waxler et al., 2000) and disengaged at school (Bethell et al., 2014).

Exposure to traumatic and chronic stress can also lead to emotional dysregulation (Dvir et al., 2014), cognitive dysfunction, and social adjustment difficulties that can impede academic success and school adjustment (Thompson, 2014). As such, educational challenges and failures can be an indicator and outcome of unmitigated stress exposure in childhood (Overstreet & Mathews, 2011). Lastly, changes or gaps in school attendance are also often a sign of distress in young students. Experiencing even one adverse childhood experience may significantly increase the likelihood of chronic absenteeism in school-age children (Stempel et al., 2017). Missing school thus serves as a signal of distress and may exacerbate the consequences of toxic stress. School personnel can support children by identifying these common signs of stress and paying attention to major changes in children's behaviors as possible indicators of distress.

4.2.2 School Refusal as a Sign of Stress

For some children, school itself can be a major stressor, particularly if they have learning difficulties or special educational needs, poor interactions with peers or teachers, or anxiety in new social settings (Kearney, 2008). Common signs of school-based stress include frequent complaints about school, negative emotional responses to school-related topics, and school phobia and refusal in more severe circumstances (Kearney, 2003). School refusal occurs when a child is emotionally distressed about attending school, typically manifesting as anxiety and depressive reactions, and thus refuses to attend or stay in school for the whole day (Fremont, 2003; King & Bernstein, 2001). Motivations for school refusal are thought to include anxiety-related avoidance of negative school-based stimuli or situations, and desires to solicit attention from adults or support from school personnel (Kearney, 2008). In young children, school refusal frequently manifests as emotional outbursts or somatic complaints when preparing to go to school or during the school day. Some research suggests that school refusal behaviors peak around the ages of 5 to 6 and 10 to 11 years old and occur more commonly around school transitions (Tyrrell, 2005).

4.3 School-based Solutions for Stress

Although school can be a source of stress, it can also be a vehicle for teaching children coping skills at scale and providing them with opportunities to practice coping skills.

4.3.1 School-based Stress Interventions

Social and Emotional Learning (SEL) is the umbrella term that captures the process of developing skills necessary for productive emotion management and social engagement (Jones & Doolittle, 2017). SEL skills encompass a wide range of cognitive and social processes that are often demonstrated and measured in terms of emotional and social competencies such as self-regulation, emotional awareness, and social problem-solving skills (Humphrey et al., 2011). These skills are cultivated at home and in school (Jones & Doolittle, 2017) and predict better school adjustment and success (Raver, 2002). SEL programs in schools have been cited as an effective universal strategy for helping young students develop emotional competencies and improve adaptive outcomes (Humphrey et al., 2011; Pandey et al., 2018; Payton et al., 2008). SEL programs are also evidenced to support crucial skills for coping with stress in preschoolers (Pang et al., 2018) and elementary students (Schonert-Reichl et al., 2015).

Programs that focus on mindfulness-based stress reduction have become a popular subgroup of SEL approaches for cultivating stress resilience and promoting emotion regulation skills in school (Meiklejohn et al., 2012). Although evidence for the effectiveness of mindfulness interventions has been mixed (Pandey et al., 2018), largely due to the wide variety of programs and implementation strategies and the challenge of getting children to practice the newly learned skills on a regular basis, some studies show meaningful improvements in children's stress compared to non-treatment control groups (Dunning et al., 2022) and reductions in cortisol following school-based mindfulness interventions (Carro et al., 2023). Intervention efforts may provide effective solutions for target groups, but the structure and pedagogical practice of the school can promote well-being and stress resilience for the educational ecosystem more broadly.

4.3.2 Structuring Schools to Support Resilience to Stress

Trauma-informed, *trauma-responsive*, and *trauma-sensitive* are terms frequently used, often interchangeably, to describe frameworks designed to address the impacts of early adversity and toxic stress in schools. Broadly speaking, trauma-informed practices in education are intended to shift perspectives from pathologizing the child to encouraging empathy and understanding of the ways in which traumatic and stressful experiences inform children's behavior (Thomas et al., 2019). Approaches to trauma-informed education vary greatly. School-based trauma-informed practices range from promoting well-being and stress prevention to responding directly to traumatized children to support healing from adverse experiences. Evidence for the effectiveness of trauma-informed practice has been mixed and is still emerging, largely due to the disparate methods of delivery and the wide variety of programs offered (Thomas et al., 2019). One meta-analysis of 21 studies examining teacher-delivered trauma-informed programming found significant improvements in students' traumatic stress symptoms and educator knowledge of the impacts of traumatic stress (Cafaro et al., 2023). Still, important critiques of trauma-informed education highlight how the framework has been impactful yet imperfect.

Critics posit that overemphasizing a child's traumatic experiences may reinforce a deficit narrative that can cause more harm by pathologizing children as traumatized and deflecting attention away from the role of the school context (Cafaro et al., 2023; Ginwright, 2021; Haynes et al., 2023). *Healing-centered engagement* offers a powerful asset-based alternative to the traditional trauma-informed approach. Ginwright (2021) argued that trauma and healing happen simultaneously, and thus, educational practice must go beyond diagnosing and treating symptoms of trauma to cultivate learning environments that promote student wellness and foster resilience. This framework is rooted in the understanding that stress and trauma exist as a function of the environment, particularly environments that are oppressive, unjust, and inequitable. Resilience to stress and healing in those contexts require healthy identity development, community belongingness, healthy adults engaging with the children, and a collective emphasis on well-being (Ginwright, 2021).

4.4 Practical Considerations for Combating School-based Stress

School may not be stressful for all children, but all children deserve the opportunity to learn, grow, and develop unencumbered by school–based stress. Educational practitioners can promote learning by reducing stressors in their schools and recognizing the symptoms of stress when they arise as opportunities to foster children's resilience and coping. Alleviating school-based stress and equipping children with the skills to adapt in the face of stress also require a reimagining of the school context that centers student and educator well-being. Researchers aspiring to contribute to children's stress resilience in schools can expand on efforts to examine the effectiveness of interventions and structural school-based solutions, with particular attention paid to unpacking how stress physiology interacts with child functioning in school (Obradović & Armstrong-Carter, 2020).

5 The Role of Neighborhoods in Stress and Resilience

"It takes a village" is a phrase colloquially referenced in conversations about rearing children. In modern times, the village is the neighborhood, a space for positive interactions and enriching activities outside the home, or a violent area that triggers continuous vigilance and engenders toxic stress. Growing up in a dangerous neighborhood can have direct effects on children, such as being a victim of crimes, and indirect effects, such as obesity due to reduced opportunities for outdoor physical activity (Thakur et al., 2020; Ye et al., 2023). Neighborhood stressors may be forms of disadvantage such as low levels of socioeconomic resources (e.g., limited access to nutrient-dense foods; Conrey et al., 2022), low cohesion amongst community members (Fleckman et al., 2022), and lack of access to outdoor activities (Morgan Hughey et al., 2017). This Section highlights empirical evidence on the impacts of neighborhood stressors on child development and sources of resilience that stem from having support in neighborhood communities.

5.1 Neighborhood Stressors

5.1.1 Neighborhood Violence and Safety Concerns

Witnessing violence in the neighborhood and being a victim of violence are stressful events for children. In the longer term, repeated instances of direct victimization and exposure to violence in the neighborhood may constitute chronic stress for children. Developmental scientists and clinicians increasingly recognize the significance of these risk pathways and have taken steps to capture community-level stressors in measurements of adverse childhood experiences (Thakur et al., 2020; Ye et al., 2023). One example is the Pediatric ACEs and Related Life Events screener, which specifically asks whether the child has seen, heard, or been a victim of violence in their neighborhood or community (Thakur et al., 2020), in addition to the original ten adversities from the landmark ACE Study (Felitti et al., 1998). Of 367 children aged 3 months to 11 years from a low-income population, 24.4 percent endorsed neighborhood violence as a life event, making it the fourth highest in prevalence in that sample, after caregiver mental illness, domestic violence, and divorce (Thakur et al., 2020). Importantly, neighborhood violence does not act in isolation to confer risk for children's maladaptive developmental trajectories, as those who experience neighborhood violence have a 90.4 percent chance of experiencing one of the other ACEs, and 73.5 percent of experiencing two (Thakur et al., 2020). Additionally, neighborhood violence often acts in concert with other sources of stress. Living in a neighborhood with limited play opportunities, poor cohesion among community members, high levels of socioeconomic disadvantage, and inadequate access to nutrient-rich foods may also compound stress for children.

Neighborhood stressors can elevate risks for mental and physical health problems in children (Shonkoff & Phillips, 2000). For example, living in an unsafe and dangerous neighborhood is associated with a variety of academic, behavioral, and clinical problems (Shonkoff & Phillips, 2000), and more recent exposure may be more impactful compared to past exposure (Coley et al., 2015). In urban children, community violence is associated with heightened asthma risk (Sternthal et al., 2010), perhaps due to a stress-induced inflammatory signaling pathway (Chen et al., 2019). Additionally, children living in neighborhoods with greater severity of crime and social disorder have heightened externalizing and total behavioral problems (Fleckman et al., 2022; Maschi et al., 2010). Children's unique experiences with violence (i.e., witnessing violence versus direct victimization) may differentially impact their health and well-being. Witnessing violence increases children's risk for depression, anxiety, cognitive impairment, and aggression (Aisenberg & Herrenkohl, 2008). Being a victim of community violence, along with low perceptions of neighborhood safety, is associated with more reports of behavioral problems in 5- to 11-year-old children (Maschi et al., 2010) – which was not observed in children who witnessed community violence but were not direct victims. Similarly, children whose parents perceive their neighborhood as being less safe may spend more time in sedentary indoor activities such as watching television, which in turn may increase their risk of being overweight (Cecil-Karb & Grogan-Kaylor, 2009). Access to a safe environment to engage in normative developmental activities like play and other physical activities is important for children's health.

Safety concerns for children and families are often captured by various measures, and these unsafe neighborhood characteristics have important implications for health-related outcomes. Five- to 18-year-olds living in neighborhoods with higher poverty or crime levels had higher levels of serum C-reactive protein, a marker of systemic inflammation, compared to children in neighborhoods with low rates of poverty and crime (Broyles et al., 2012). In a study investigating neighborhood characteristics, 5- to 16-year-old children who live in proximity to liquor stores (where inebriated individuals congregate) were less likely to show a complete recovery to baseline in their cortisol response after an acute laboratory stressor (Theall et al., 2017). Children living in neighborhoods with high rates of reported domestic violence and violent crimes also showed incomplete cortisol recovery responses to the acute laboratory stressor (Theall et al., 2017). Furthermore, these adverse neighborhood characteristics were also significantly associated with shorter telomere length, a marker of accelerated biological aging (Theall et al., 2017).

Adversity in the social context, marked by neighborhood violence and whether the child experienced discrimination, housing insecurity, or food insecurity, is associated with poorer general and behavioral health (Ye et al., 2023). Here, headaches, eczema, and somatic symptoms were uniquely associated with exposure to adverse social contexts but not maltreatment or household challenges (Ye et al., 2023). Neighborhood disadvantages, such as lack of safety, are associated with environmental deprivations such as poor housing conditions and household pollution (Ciula & Skinner, 2015). This may serve as an additional pathway through which children experience an increased risk for somatic symptoms, particularly if they have limited access to safe outdoor activities and spend more time in homes that have greater deterioration and more safety hazards (Evans, 2004).

Neighborhood stressors can also make it difficult for children to focus while at school and perform well on examinations. Children who are exposed to violent crimes perform worse on language arts tests, with chronic neighborhood violence being the most harmful to children's performance (Schwartz et al., 2022). These experiences of academic failure and hindered school performance could also be a source of stress for children. Exposure to crime is associated with poor academic performance (Schwartz et al., 2022). Chronic exposure to violent crimes in their neighborhoods has lasting effects on children's academic outcomes, lowering test scores (Schwartz et al., 2022). In elementary school-aged children, neighborhood violence exposure is associated with poorer academic achievement (Milam et al., 2010). However, this association was no longer significant after controlling for self-reported safety walking to and from school and the percentage of students receiving free and reduced-price lunches (Milam et al., 2010). These findings suggest that household economic disadvantage and perceived lack of safety may explain a significant portion of the association between neighborhood violence and academic achievement.

5.1.2 Neighborhood Poverty and Socioeconomic Deprivation

Exposure to chronic stressors can shape children's psychobiological stress response systems (Johnston-Brooks et al., 1998), conferring risks for poorer health and overall well-being. In the neighborhood, the low economic status and lack of access to resources are forms of chronic stressors for children. For example, children living in neighborhoods replete with high poverty, high unemployment, and inadequate housing are more likely to live in crowded (i.e., high-density) homes (Evans, 2004). Greater household density, a form of environmental stress, is associated with exaggerated cardiovascular responses to acute stressors for children, which is in turn positively associated with the number of school days missed due to illness (Johnston-Brooks et al., 1998). Compared to children who live in affluent neighborhoods, children who live in neighborhoods with more low-income neighbors are more likely to exhibit higher externalizing problems (Duncan et al., 1994).

Poverty often co-occurs with neighborhood deprivation, impacting children's well-being in multiple ways (Ciula & Skinner, 2015). Low neighborhood opportunity, measured by indicators of education, health, environmental, social, and economic opportunity based on home address, interacts with family SES to influence children's daily cortisol levels and physical health (Roubinov et al., 2018). Specifically, when beginning school for the first time, kindergarten-aged children in neighborhoods with low opportunity and from low-SES families had higher levels of daily cortisol output, which could be a marker for heightened HPA axis arousal (Roubinov et al., 2018). By the end of the first school year, for the children who lived in low-opportunity neighborhoods, being from a low-SES family was associated with poorer general health outcomes. Importantly, family SES is not predictive of spring semester health for children who live in high-opportunity neighborhoods (Roubinov et al., 2018). Taken together, these studies suggest that exposure to violence in the neighborhood, having few resources in the community, and living in a neighborhood with spaces that have a higher incidence of criminal activity are aspects of neighborhood disadvantage that can "get under the skin" to shape biological processes and risks for poorer physical health. Distressing childhood neighborhood conditions also have lasting negative effects on health outcomes into adulthood, such as cardiovascular disease, depression, and obesity (Jutte et al., 2015).

Neighborhood socioeconomic deprivation, environmental characteristics (e.g., poor housing conditions, litter on streets), and safety concerns (e.g., violence, crime) have impacts on infants and children such that worse neighborhood conditions are associated with more sleep problems (Mackinnon et al., 2020; Singh & Kenney, 2013). Sleep duration and quality are critically important in shaping children's physiology and health outcomes through various restorative biological processes that occur during sleep (Bathory & Tomopoulos, 2017). Consequently, poor sleep may have detrimental effects on children's physiology and disruptions in children's and families' daily lives and routines.

Relatedly, neighborhood deprivation was associated with teacher-reported conduct problems in a sample of 10-year-old children (Galán et al., 2017). Neighborhood material deprivation (e.g., low SES, limited access to healthcare, high poverty, and housing insecurity) has been associated with a higher risk for obesity for children as young as 2 years old (Conrey et al., 2022). This may be in part due to the lack of readily available healthy food choices – living in food deserts – which has been linked to a higher risk for obesity in elementary school-aged children (Thomsen et al., 2016). For children and families living in food deserts, the lack of access to healthy and affordable food, as well as the additional processes (e.g., traveling miles from home) to obtain food may be a direct source of stress, contributing to declining physical and mental well-being (Crowe et al., 2018).

5.1.3 Social Stressors in Disadvantaged Neighborhoods

Aside from objective neighborhood characteristics such as poverty and crime rates, how people perceive their neighborhoods is critical to their well-being. Children living in neighborhoods with greater social cohesion and better physical conditions enjoy more hours of outdoor play and spend fewer hours watching television, all of which are associated with lower child body mass index (BMI) (Kimbro et al., 2011). Living in environments where the community members feel close to and supportive of each other may be critical in nurturing safe spaces for children to engage in activities that foster good health.

On the flip side, higher levels of neighborhood disorder – neighborhood social problems such as drug dealing and gang activity – are associated with higher levels of childhood adversity which, in turn, are associated with poorer child behavioral outcomes, such as higher levels of aggression, depression, anxiety, withdrawal, and attention problems years later (Wang & Maguire-Jack, 2018). Furthermore, indices of neighborhood disorder were all separately and significantly associated with a heightened risk for behavioral problems in children.

Neighborhood conditions differ not only based on SES, but also ethnicity. Children of color are more likely to live in high-poverty and under-resourced neighborhoods compared to European American children (Drake & Rank, 2009). Moreover, African American and European American families of similar socioeconomic backgrounds do not reside in similarly resourced neighborhoods – African American families of high SES often reside in under-resourced neighborhoods (Intrator et al., 2016). Historical practices like residential segregation have affected children in areas such as education, medical services, and psychological well-being (Shonkoff et al., 2021). Emerging studies also show that interpersonal discrimination, such as unfair treatment due to group membership, has also been linked to negative health effects in children (Shonkoff et al., 2021).

5.2 Neighborhood Sources of Resilience

In the context of ongoing chronic stressors, positive aspects of neighborhoods may help boost children's resilience. For example, living in neighborhoods with high social cohesion and high informal social control (i.e., a high likelihood of people in the neighborhood taking action against threats within the community) are factors associated with resilience for children experiencing maltreatment, defined as exhibiting low levels of teacher-reported antisocial behavior at ages 5 and 7, despite being maltreated (Jaffee et al., 2007). As such, policy initiatives are needed to increase safety and economic resources within neighborhoods (for a discussion, see Parenteau et al., 2023).

5.2.1 Play and Extracurricular Activities

Children's interactions with peers through play may reduce their stress levels. For instance, participation in free play can influence physiological regulation. Children with more opportunities for free play within the previous week demonstrated better regulation of the ANS in one study (Gleason et al., 2021). Because play has been linked to a better mood and lower levels of allostatic load (Burdette & Whitaker, 2005), having ample play opportunities may facilitate stress regulation in children.

Additionally, participation in extracurricular activities has been associated with many positive outcomes. Particularly, engagement in sports has unique benefits for older children (P. A. Harrison & Narayan, 2003). Some benefits include being more likely to attend school, engage in healthy behaviors, and have higher self-esteem. Simply being involved in sports was linked to fewer reports of psychological difficulties such as feelings of sadness, anxiety, and suicidal ideation (P. A. Harrison & Narayan, 2003).

Interventions that improve neighborhood resources by expanding green spaces, bolstering positive and healthy social activity in the neighborhood, and cleaning up the environment have shown promise in mitigating violence (Aiyer et al., 2015; Hohl et al., 2019). A study with 7-year-old children found that green space accessibility was associated with lower allostatic load, a marker of multisystem stress dysregulation (Ribeiro et al., 2019). For children and younger teenagers, interaction with nature reduces stress, promotes stress resilience, and improves mental well-being (Tillmann et al., 2018). In line with prevention efforts aiming to improve neighborhoods by cleaning and adding greenery to the streets to promote safer neighborhoods (Hohl et al., 2019), increasing access to nature and green spaces may have a direct effect on children's mental health outcomes in the context of stress. Residential proximity to outdoor and green play spaces, along with greater diversity of play opportunities, were associated with a lower prevalence of psychological disorders in a study of children ages 0–12. (Pérez-del-Pulgar et al., 2021). Furthermore, children suffering from chronic illnesses seem to benefit from play, showing greater adaptability to illness-related stressors (Nijhof et al., 2018). Although an emerging area of research, these initial studies suggest that play is a form of positive, healthy social activity.

5.2.2 Interpersonal Stress-Buffering Mechanisms in the Community

In the context of neighborhood stressors, interpersonal relationships that provide support and cohesion may improve children's outcomes across multiple developmental domains. Collective efficacy within the neighborhood can provide protection and buffer children from the negative impacts of exposure to community violence (Aisenberg & Herrenkohl, 2008). For children who experience chronic stressors at home, having strong interpersonal relationships in the community can be beneficial for increasing belonging and connectedness, which will promote healthier developmental outcomes (Isumi et al., 2023). Additionally, studies have shown that neighborhood cohesion is associated with lower rates of child neglect (Maguire-Jack & Showalter, 2016; McLeigh et al., 2018).

In a sample of families with a child with autism, having strong neighborhood support was associated with higher family resilience (Menezes et al., 2023). Having a child with autism can be a major stressor for families as they navigate structural challenges to meet the unique developmental needs of their child. Having neighbors who are helpful and share knowledge can mitigate stressors for these families (Menezes et al., 2023). Additionally, supportive and high-quality relationships with adults in the community or neighborhood can also protect children from ongoing stressors and adversities. In sum, neighborhoods and communities can also be sources of protection and resilience against stress in childhood.

6 Discrimination Stress and Cultural Sources of Resilience

"Why are all the black kids sitting together in the cafeteria?" This question, posed by Tatum (1997), has been asked by children and adults alike across US schools. Tatum discussed stressors faced by children of color due to discrimination and how affinity groups based on ethnicity[1] can offer a safe space to discuss common challenges, thereby serving as protective factors for youth of color. This Section discusses discrimination-related stress and cultural sources of resilience for minoritized children.

6.1 Discrimination as a Source of Stress

6.1.1 What is Discrimination?

Discrimination has been defined as unfair treatment based on one's identity (Benner & Graham, 2013) and has been identified as a major source of stress (Adam et al., 2020; Levy et al., 2016). Children can experience many forms of

---

[1] Guidelines for best practices when studying diverse groups recommend against using the term "race" to avoid perpetuating stereotypes about the biological nature of race and promote using the term "ethnicity" as a more precise and descriptive term for describing groups that differ based on cultural and social factors (Burlew et al., 2019; Causadias et al., 2018). As such, we avoid using the term "race" except in specific instances where we describe research studies that studied participants' understanding of racial categories or racial discrimination. [Burlew, A. K., Peteet, B. J., McCuistian, C., & Miller-Roenigk, B. D. (2019). Best practices for researching diverse groups. *American Journal of Orthopsychiatry, 89*(3), 354–368; Causadias, J. M., Vitriol, J. A., & Atkin, A. L. (2018). Do we overemphasize the role of culture in the behavior of racial/ethnic minorities? Evidence of a cultural (mis)attribution bias in American psychology. *American Psychologist, 73*(3), 243–255]

discrimination in their daily lives, based on multiple aspects of their identity (e.g., ethnicity, gender, immigration status). Children of color are more likely to experience discrimination due to minority status. By age 6, children can sort others into racial and cultural categories (Pauker et al., 2016); children as young as 7 can recognize discrimination (Marcelo & Yates, 2019). As of 2023, over half of children in United States are children of color (Children's Defense Fund, 2023), thereby highlighting the high prevalence of potential experiences of discrimination in countries with children from diverse backgrounds.

6.1.2 Theoretical Frameworks

Cross-cultural interpretations of discrimination vary, and anti-discrimination laws differ from country to country, likely shaping how children from different age groups in various geographic regions perceive discrimination (Liu & Cimpian, 2025). Nonetheless, several theoretical frameworks have aimed to explain the impact of discrimination on mental health and well-being. For instance, the *race-based disparities in stress and sleep in context* (RDSSC; Levy et al., 2016) model proposed that discrimination is interpreted as a social threat by one's stress-response systems and can, in turn, influence other outcomes such as cognitive functioning and academic performance. Spencer et al.'s (1997) *phenomenological variant of ecological systems theory* (PVEST) is used to understand the unique stressors faced by ethnic minorities (Spencer et al., 1997). It is a conceptual framework that describes how interactions within the immediate environment – specifically related to sex, social class, ethnic background, skin color, and differences in maturation – are nested inside larger social systems and in turn influence one's repetitive feedback responses, crystalizing into personality and identity (Spencer et al., 1997). Another framework used to understand discrimination is the *minority stress model*, which explains that persons from stigmatized groups experience excess stress due to their minority social position (Meyer, 2003). For example, those who belong to a minority group may encounter dominant social norms that are mismatched to their identity, and their social interactions may expose them to negative stereotypes about their group that may become internalized, causing distress (Meyer, 2003).

Discrimination can occur in many ways, having negative impacts on a variety of child health outcomes, including blood pressure, obesity, inflammation, and somatic symptoms (Priest et al., 2013, 2024). The term "institutional discrimination" has been used to describe discrimination-related experiences embedded within political, economic, social, and healthcare systems and has been linked to disparities in toxin exposure (e.g., contaminated water, air pollution) and in the rate of adverse experiences affecting children's development (Shonkoff et al., 2021). Daily experiences of discrimination that occur between individuals, otherwise described as interpersonal discrimination, further perpetuate structural racism and influence children's health (Shonkoff et al., 2021).

6.1.3 The Impact of Discrimination Stress

The literature on the impact of discrimination stress on children, particularly children of color, is limited (but see Priest et al., 2013, 2024). A major barrier to understanding the effects of racial and ethnic discrimination-related stress in children is the lack of measures (Braddock et al., 2021). Despite these issues, a scoping review found that racial discrimination was linked to anxiety and depression in children and adolescents (Braddock et al., 2021). Even the perception of discrimination has been found to contribute to poorer mental health in a study of Puerto Rican children and adolescents (Szalacha et al., 2003). Importantly, it is vital to understand how younger children perceive discriminatory acts (Liu & Cimpian, 2025) as children's physiological systems can be especially sensitive to the potential outcomes from early discrimination-related stressor exposure (Shonkoff et al., 2021).

It is unlikely that exposure to a single discrimination-stressor event increases risk for detrimental stress outcomes in children, including children of marginalized identities. However, exposure to repeated individual incidents could activate stress-response systems. As such, unpredictable and uncontrollable discrimination-related stressors can accumulate into detrimental outcomes over time, such as poorer physical health outcomes, biological aging, and accelerated pubertal development in children. For instance, a large, nationally representative study of 11,235 US children who were 9 to 10 years old showed advanced pubertal development linked to experiences of discrimination and higher suicidality rates in African American youth compared to non-African American youth, after accounting for other types of adversities (Argabright et al., 2022).

Notably, emerging research also illuminates the complexity of discrimination-related stress exposure in children. Younger children (ages 4–9) from the United States were more likely to rate discriminatory actions as justified compared to identical actions driven by other motives when compared to adults (Liu & Cimpian, 2025). This can be problematic, as it may lead them to engage in discrimination, perpetuating unjust cultural norms. This finding also highlights an opportunity for developing effective interventions for each developmental period.

While these findings underscore the need for tailored interventions, a recurrent issue is that studies investigating discrimination often lump together various ethnic subgroups (Burlew et al., 2019). There are limited measures to account for how group identity contributes to children's perceived stress and stress response outcomes (Braddock et al., 2021). Thus, research has so far not fully captured how discrimination experiences impact minority children's stress and resilience. Future research should examine discrimination stress through a developmental lens to understand how children of color manage stress and attain resilience against discrimination experiences (Szalacha et al., 2003). Specifically, it is crucial to capture discrimination frequency, severity, and duration (Williams et al., 2019).

6.2 Cultural Sources of Resilience

For children of color, having a sense of belonging in peer groups who share similarities in ethnic identity can help buffer against stressors related to peer relationships. As seen in longitudinal studies with African American youth as young as 10 years old, experiences of discrimination lead to fewer depressive symptoms among children who affiliate with prosocial peers (Brody et al., 2006).

Maintaining a connection with one's ethnic heritage can also serve as a cultural asset for ethnic minority youth (Gaylord-Harden et al., 2012). Children as young as 7 who report a stronger sense of belonging to their racial and ethnic identity group experience reduced negative effects of discrimination on adjustment behaviors, such as internalizing and externalizing symptoms (Marcelo & Yates, 2019). Additionally, a strong sense of racial-ethnic identity can serve as a protective factor that promotes emotional and behavioral health, as well as academic success (Austin et al., 2022).

Culturally relevant coping strategies can also promote resilience. Although many African American youth experience discrimination, not all experience deleterious mental health outcomes, largely due to cultural assets and lessons from their community about coping with these stressors (Gaylord-Harden et al., 2012). Culturally relevant coping rooted in common practices from their communities is likely beneficial because it can encourage communication, elicit positive social support, and facilitate access to positive adult mentors.

In summary, identity-based discrimination can activate one's stress response systems, such as the HPA axis (Adam et al., 2020; Priest et al., 2024; Shonkoff et al., 2021). Researchers can engage in culturally informed training at all stages of their research to contribute to more culturally relevant outcomes (Burlew et al., 2019). Considering how parental ethnic socialization practices can influence their child's identity development can provide insight on how to develop more effective interventions (Huguley et al., 2019). Additionally, educators and community leaders are integral to teaching children not to discriminate against others, along with educating children of color on how to navigate prejudice and discrimination by helping them cultivate pride in their identity (Marcelo & Yates, 2019). Programs and policies aimed at bolstering children's pride in their racial-ethnic identity may help to reduce the negative effects of discrimination. Finally, culturally relevant interventions and extracurricular activities that offer positive and appropriate opportunities, such as making friends, developing social skills, and exploring their commitment to education, can buffer stress and promote long-term resilience for all children.

7 Stress, Trauma, and Mental Health Interventions

"Young children are the most vulnerable to adversity, but they also have the greatest capacity for healing when the interventions are begun early," according to Harris (2018, p. 146), a pediatrician and former Surgeon General of California who championed state-wide initiatives that screen for, prevent, and treat the effects of childhood adversity. Although exposure to chronic and traumatic stress can increase the risk of countless short- and long-term mental health problems, several evidence-based interventions and mental health treatments are available to address symptoms resulting from chronic and traumatic stress. This Section first clarifies similarities and differences between stress and trauma. Next, it reviews literature on the connection between stress or trauma and mental health outcomes such as depression, anxiety, PTSD, and disruptive behavior. It also discusses the common misdiagnosis of trauma reactions as different disorders and the diagnosis of complex post-traumatic stress disorder (C-PTSD). Finally, the majority of this Section reviews evidence-based interventions for preventing and treating stress and trauma in childhood.

7.1 Trauma and Stress

There is a complex relation between the terms stress and trauma. As previously discussed, stress is defined as a threat to the physical or mental integrity of an individual, especially when situations include unpredictability and uncontrollability. Stress can range from minor everyday stress (e.g., daily hassles) to toxic (chronic, severe and unbuffered by a caregiver) or traumatic stress (in response to a traumatic event – an event that threatens the life or sense of self of an individual, either an acute event like a motor vehicle accident, or a chronic stressor, such as physical abuse). Toxic and traumatic stress are overlapping yet not synonymous concepts, but both overwhelm a child's coping capability and can lead to detrimental outcomes. Traumas are, by definition, stressful, whereas stressors are not all considered traumatic.

7.2 Stress, Trauma, and Mental Health

Stress caused by trauma is one of the leading causes of mental illness in childhood (Kessler et al., 2010). Early-life stress (i.e., stress in the first 5 years) appears to be especially impactful in increasing the risk of mental illness (Humphreys & Zeanah, 2015). A review, which combined the results of 68 systematic reviews and meta-analyses, reported that experiencing stressful events in childhood (as opposed to adulthood) is linked to increased risk of internalizing symptoms (including withdrawal, sadness, worries, low self-esteem, and somatic symptoms such as headaches and stomachaches), depressive disorders, anxiety disorders, and suicidality (Sahle et al., 2022). Other studies have reported an increased risk of externalizing symptoms, including disruptive behavior, aggression, criminal offending, and substance abuse (Muniz et al., 2019). Stress in the absence of a supportive caregiver to buffer stress, such as in the case of emotional abuse, tends to be the most significant predictor of multiple negative outcomes (Muniz et al., 2019). In a group of treatment-seeking preschool-aged children (Crusto et al., 2010), experiences of stress and trauma were nearly ubiquitous, with most children experiencing multiple types of adversity (e.g., witnessing domestic violence, separation from a caregiver, maltreatment). Thus, experiences of stress and trauma account for a significant portion of the burden of mental illness in childhood.

Researchers have examined various mechanisms of these associations. At the biological level, the HPA axis has been implicated in the association between stress and mental and physical health (Gunnar et al., 2015). Specific structural and functional brain changes are associated with early-life stress that may lead to vulnerability to mental illness (Herzberg & Gunnar, 2020; McLaughlin et al., 2019). The majority of studies on early-life adversity and neural development find lower amygdala, medial prefrontal cortex, and hippocampal volume and greater amygdala activation to threat among children exposed to more adversity (McLaughlin et al., 2019). One randomized controlled trial conducted in Romania, the Bucharest Early Intervention Project, found reduced cortical gray matter volume among children who had experienced institutionalization compared to those reared in their birth families (Sheridan et al., 2012). Epigenetic pathways (i.e., environmentally mediated changes in gene expression) have also been proposed as a way that stress "gets under the skin" to influence later development (Cheng et al., 2022). On the psychological level, several processes have been investigated as potential mediators of the associations between early life stress and mental illness. Difficulties with emotion regulation have been identified as a general risk factor for psychopathology that is impacted by early-life stress (Miu et al., 2022). Difficulties with broader self-regulation and executive functioning have also been implicated as a potential pathway to developing mental illness, especially from experiences of deprivation and neglect (Sheridan et al., 2017). Experiences of stress and trauma also affect how individuals process rewards (Novick et al., 2018), how they appraise situations (Aafjes-van Doorn et al., 2020), how they identify and understand emotions (Doretto & Scivoletto, 2018), and how they form relationships (Doyle & Cicchetti, 2017), starting in childhood. Several of these mechanisms have become targets of interventions, as discussed later.

A common misconception is the incorrect assumption that experiences of trauma result only in PTSD. PTSD is defined by three main symptoms: reexperiencing the traumatic event(s), avoidance of trauma reminders, and a sense of current threat. As reviewed earlier, trauma and other adversities are associated with an increased risk of a wide range of mental health concerns, not just PTSD. However, for some conditions (e.g., attention deficit hyperactivity disorder, oppositional defiant disorder), debate exists among scholars as to whether trauma increases the risk of these disorders or whether trauma reactions are being misdiagnosed as conduct or attention problems (Szymanski et al., 2011). Often, symptoms of a trauma reaction mimic other disorders, including difficulty concentrating, difficulty regulating emotions, and irritability. This can lead to an under-diagnosis of PTSD in populations experiencing significant trauma and stress, such as maltreated children (Grasso et al., 2009).

Trauma reactions can also be comorbid with other conditions, complicating the diagnostic picture. The ICD-11 (World Health Organization, 2019) includes a diagnosis of complex PTSD, which attempts to address issues of comorbidity and misdiagnosis (Maercker, 2021). Complex PTSD is defined by the three "classic" PTSD symptoms and by three additional symptoms common in individuals who have been exposed to chronic, inescapable trauma such as child maltreatment, domestic violence, or torture: emotion regulation difficulties (e.g., problems calming down when upset), relationship difficulties (e.g., difficulties trusting and forming relationships), and negative self-concept (e.g., beliefs about the self as a failure or unlovable; Brewin et al., 2017). These constructs overlap with several of the potential mediating mechanisms described earlier, linking stress and trauma with other forms of mental illness. It is not surprising that many empirically supported treatments for stress/trauma-related disorders and transdiagnostic treatments focus on targeting these symptoms. The remainder of this Section describes therapeutic approaches to prevent trauma and support children who have experienced stress.

7.3 Interventions for Stress and Trauma

Numerous interventions address the repercussions of stress and trauma in children, as well as interventions designed to prevent stress and trauma from occurring in the first place. The US-based National Child Traumatic Stress Network (2024b) and California Evidence-Based Clearinghouse for Child Welfare (2025) each maintains a list of empirically supported treatments that address stress and trauma. In line with the public health model of primary, secondary, and tertiary prevention, there are universal evidence-based interventions (Tier 1) that aim to prevent stress and trauma before they occur and interrupt the intergenerational transmission of trauma from parents to children. There are also targeted approaches (Tier 2) for children and families experiencing stressors (e.g., poverty, violence, parental mental illness or substance use, teen pregnancy) to ameliorate the impact of stress and ideally prevent children from developing mental illness. Lastly, Tier 3 interventions include intensive, individualized interventions that are provided based on the demonstration of clinically significant symptoms or impairment. An exhaustive review is outside our scope, but this Section describes several evidence-based interventions at each tier that target stress or trauma in children aged 0 to 10 years old.

7.3.1 Systemic Population-Based Interventions

The Triple P parenting program is a systemic, population-based prevention and intervention program with five levels (societal [e.g., media campaigns], community [e.g., low-intensity seminars or parenting workshops], individual-brief [to help parents deal with common childhood behavior problems], individual-comprehensive [for moderate to severe problems], and continuing support [for specific risk factors or ongoing support]). The individual-comprehensive level of Triple P is independently effective at improving parenting, reducing disruptive behaviors, and improving children's socioemotional outcomes (Sanders et al., 2014). The Triple P system as a whole also has demonstrated population-level decreases in child maltreatment and out-of-home placements (Prinz et al., 2009).

7.3.2 Tier 1 and 2 Home Visiting Interventions

At the universal prevention and targeted levels of intervention, evidence-based programs tend to be offered in the perinatal or early childhood period and often meet children and families where they are, such as in the home, at the pediatricians' office, or in schools. Home visiting programs have been established for many decades, initially targeting infant physical health and survival (e.g., 1937 home visiting in Denmark; Hjort et al., 2017), and then shifting increasingly toward mental health and well-being over the last several decades (e.g., Michigan Model of Infant Mental Health Home Visiting [MI-IMH-HV] established in the 1970s; Weatherston et al., 2020). Long-established universal home visiting programs, such as those found in the Nordic countries, are continuing to add emphasis on reducing stress and promoting socioemotional well-being in addition to traditional content such as nutrition and safety (Daníelsdóttir & Ingudóttir, 2020). More countries are moving toward implementation of universal home visiting programs in hopes of preventing stress for families and promoting children's optimal development (e.g., Khang et al., 2022). Universal programs have the benefits of reducing the stigma of participating in services and promoting well-being in all children, even in the absence of notable risk factors.

Family Connects (Dodge et al., 2013) is one U.S.-based home visiting program that has been developed and implemented as a universal intervention available to all families of newborn infants in a southern US county. This brief intervention (1 to 3 visits) was effective at engaging families and reducing child maltreatment reports and hospital visits (Goodman et al., 2021). While the United States is far from national implementation, numerous evidence-based programs designed to prevent stress and trauma have been disseminated in different regions. Healthy Families America (Harding et al., 2007) was established as an effective state-wide program for preventing child maltreatment through universal screening for risk factors and provision of intensive home-based services for families in need. Other programs (such as the Nurse Family Partnership; Olds, 2006) are targeted at first-time mothers living in poverty in hopes of buffering children from the stressors of financial hardship and related disruptions in parenting. The effects of such preventative interventions are both cost-effective and long-lasting (Olds et al., 2019). Several targeted interventions are designed to work with families that have already been exposed to trauma, such as intimate partner violence, mental health issues, substance use disorder, and child welfare system involvement. Attachment and Biobehavioral Catch Up (Dozier et al., 2006), Promoting First Relationships (Oxford et al., 2021), Child First (Lowell et al., 2011), and MI-IMH-HV (Riggs et al., 2022) are all targeted home visiting programs that buffer children from stressors and prevent negative developmental outcomes. Most of these interventions target sensitive parenting and promote secure attachment to the primary caregiver as a means of buffering stress and trauma.

7.3.3 Tier 1 and Tier 2 Integrated Interventions

Some Tier 1 and 2 interventions are integrated into medical centers. For example, Safe Environment for Every Kid (SEEK) is a preventative program that trains medical professionals to screen for notable risk factors for child maltreatment and other adversities and provide targeted referrals for families at heightened risk (Dubowitz et al., 2009). The program also uses principles of motivational interviewing, a brief intervention that promotes health change and improves engagement in the intervention. The Family Check-up intervention (Shaw et al., 2006) is designed to be integrated into a variety of settings, including primary care as well as other services such as the Women, Infants, and Children (WIC) program. This intervention is aimed at low SES families and includes motivational interviewing strategies to boost parent engagement. The intervention diverts the trajectory of disruptive behaviors when implemented in early childhood.

Schools are another common location for universal or targeted interventions. For example, Promoting Alternative Thinking Strategies (PATHS) is a universal program integrated into preschools and elementary schools that aims to reduce aggression and behavior problems and to increase emotional and social competencies (originally developed by Greenberg et al., 1995). Given its universal delivery, PATHS can reach all students, including those who have experienced stress and trauma. Although PATHS is effective at promoting socioemotional well-being overall, more intensive interventions may be needed for children with clinically elevated symptoms. For example, children who have experienced stress are more likely to display behavior problems in preschool, which puts them at risk for expulsion and may affect their entire developmental path going forward. Early Childhood Mental Health Consultation (ECMHC) is an evidence-based strategy for promoting positive development and preventing preschool expulsion in young children with disruptive behavior (Gilliam et al., 2016). In ECMHC, a mental health professional works with the childcare provider to support socioemotional well-being in the classroom as well as targeted interventions for children with evidence of clinically elevated symptoms. Similarly, the Early Risers program (August et al., 2001) aims to alter the developmental trajectory of children with early-onset aggressive behavior. It is an intensive, multicomponent intervention that involves parent-, teacher-, and child-directed interventions delivered over several years. The effects of the intervention last through high school, with youth who received the intervention showing significantly fewer symptoms of internalizing and externalizing than youth who did not receive the intervention (Hektner et al., 2014).

Other targeted (Tier 2) interventions have been developed specifically for children exposed to trauma. In elementary-aged students, Bounce Back is a cognitive-behavioral skills group intervention designed to relieve post-traumatic stress and other internalizing symptoms that are causing impairment at school (Langley et al., 2015). Adapted from the evidence-based Cognitive-Behavioral Intervention for Trauma in Schools program designed for children ages 10 to 15 (Stein et al., 2003), Bounce Back is designed for younger children (ages 5 to 11) and their caregivers. In addition to ten group sessions, each student also completes two to three individual sessions to process their personal trauma narrative and share it with their caregiver. Bounce Back reduces traumatic stress symptoms and anxiety in participating youth (Langley et al., 2015).

7.3.4 Tier 1 and Tier 2 Parent Group Interventions

Given the profound influence parents have on children's development, many evidence-based interventions are targeted at caregivers rather than children. Several targeted, empirically supported parenting groups have shown efficacy in promoting positive parent–child relationships, improving parenting, reducing child behavior problems, and buffering stress. Programs vary in their target population. Several programs target mothers at risk due to various circumstances, including substance use (e.g., Mothering from the Inside Out; Suchman et al., 2010), mental illness, or trauma history (e.g., Mom Power; Rosenblum et al., 2018). Other programs target families experiencing stress due to poverty or neighborhood violence (e.g., Chicago parent program; Gross et al., 2009). A third group of interventions targets families experiencing behavior problems (e.g., Incredible Years; Hutchings et al., 2007; Tuning into Kids; Havighurst et al., 2013), many of which have experienced stress. The Nurturing Parenting Program (Cowen, 2001) is specifically targeted at parents and their school-aged children (5 to 11 years) who have been reported to the child welfare system for maltreatment. This 15-session group program helps parents gain knowledge and skills to empower them to parent in a more positive manner.

7.3.5 Tier 3 Interventions

Tier 3 interventions consist of psychological treatments for children experiencing clinical levels of symptoms. This Section focuses on treatments specifically for children who have experienced traumatic stress and are demonstrating symptoms of a trauma reaction (for additional reviews of empirically supported treatments for child mental health issues, see Weisz & Kazdin, 2017).

Child Parent Psychotherapy (CPP; Lieberman et al., 2005) is the standard treatment for very young children (ages 0 to 5) who have experienced trauma. This dyadic intervention has common roots with infant mental health home visiting (Weatherston et al., 2020) and is based in attachment theory with psychodynamic, developmental, trauma, social learning, and cognitive behavioral influences as well. CPP's main goal is to strengthen the parent-child relationship to buffer stress and to restore and protect the child's mental health. Clinicians also use "ports of entry," meaning opportunities in the moment, to help the child and parent process their trauma through play and to support parent and child in reframing maladaptive representations of themselves and each other (Lieberman & Van Horn, 2004). They do this by speaking for the child, by pointing out connections between thoughts, feelings, and behaviors, and providing wonderings about alternative ways of interacting (Lieberman et al., 2005).

Trauma-Focused Cognitive Behavioral Therapy (TF-CBT; Cohen et al., 2006) has long been established as an empirically supported treatment for trauma in children. Originally developed and tested with children ages 7 to 13, it has been expanded to include children as young as 3. The intervention is a conjoint child and parent modular psychotherapy model, with different components completed by the parent, the child, or the parent and child together. The intervention includes multiple components, such as psychoeducation, teaching parenting skills and relaxation skills, teaching the child emotion regulation and cognitive coping, and working with the child to create a "narrative" about their trauma, including correcting any distortions in the way the child remembers the events and having the child share the narrative with their caregiver. Finally, the clinician promotes the child's future safety by providing age-appropriate education on personal and relationship safety and plans for the future following the end of treatment (Cohen et al., 2006). TF-CBT is effective at reducing trauma symptoms in a wide range of children exposed to diverse traumas (Scheeringa et al., 2011). It has also been adapted to fit various settings and cultures (O'Callaghan et al., 2013).

The Attachment, Regulation, and Competency model (Arvidson et al., 2011) uses a dyadic/familial/systems level framework and targets children exposed to complex trauma in particular. This flexible, manualized treatment targets the three titular areas of development: attachment (relationships with safe caregivers), regulation (behavioral and emotional self-regulation skills), and developmental competence (resilience across developmental systems). It too is grounded in attachment theory, with additional influences from trauma and developmental theory and science regarding resilience (Hodgdon et al., 2016). Treatment can last anywhere from twelve to fifty-two or more sessions depending on individual need. The intervention can be delivered in a variety of settings, including outpatient mental health care, home-based services, in-patient or residential services, or community locations.

7.4 Conclusions and Future Directions

While the effects of trauma and stress on children can be profound, there are numerous effective interventions for prevention and treatment. More research is needed to test the real-world effectiveness of many of these interventions, and broader dissemination of effective interventions is essential. Many interventions have demonstrated their cost-effectiveness, yet funding is still a major obstacle to wide-scale implementation. Policymakers should invest in preventing and treating stress in children, as doing so will benefit society for decades and generations to come.

8 Rearing Resilient Children

How can we rear resilient children? This question gains urgency as we consider increases in children's exposure to global stressors, such as pandemics, economic recession, climate change, natural disasters, wars and political instability, social injustice, and greater access to news about global stressors via digital media. These contextual stressors elicit the need to enhance children's coping skills and boost their capacity for resilience.

Resilience is defined as positive adaptation despite adversity and is increasingly viewed as a process rather than a stable, individual trait (Alen et al., 2024; Masten, 2018). The first waves of resilience research identified positive adaptation based on the presence of desirable behavioral, psychological, or academic outcomes among children exposed to adversity (Garmezy, 1971). Later research revealed that these beneficial outcomes can co-occur with physical health problems and biological "wear and tear", suggesting the need to broaden the definition of resilience to include indices of biological functioning and physical health (Hostinar & Miller, 2019). Because adaptation to adversity may require trade-offs between different domains of functioning (Blair & Raver, 2012), it is important to define resilience as a multidimensional construct (Luthar et al., 1993) and to assess multiple domains of functioning (e.g., behavioral, psychological, academic, social, physical health).

Resilience was initially conceived as a static, trait-level characteristic of the child, with primary emphasis on the child's own abilities to overcome hardship (Masten, 2018). Contemporary researchers view resilience differently. First, resilience is now considered a dynamic process (Masten, 2018). It is helpful to think of resilience as probabilistic, such that risk factors increase the probability of negative outcomes, and protective factors reduce the probability of negative outcomes and increase the probability of resilience whenever a child confronts a new stressor. Longitudinal studies have shown that resilience is not static or solely contained within the individual child. Instead, children exhibit resilience because of ongoing internal and external resources that are subject to change (Ungar & Theron, 2020).

Second, the growing consensus is that resilience is multidimensional and outcome-specific, such that many individuals exposed to early adversity may show positive adaptation in one domain (e.g., cognitive, social-emotional) while showing deficits in another, such as physical health (Hostinar & Miller, 2019). Because of the multidimensional nature of resilience, instead of describing an individual as exhibiting general resilience, it is more appropriate to discuss resilience in relation to the specific dimension measured (e.g., resilience in the emotional, social, or physical domain).

Third, resilience depends on bidirectional relations among multiple aspects of both the environment and the individual. Increasing emphasis has been placed on supportive close relationships, including parents or caregivers (see Section 2), peers (see Section 3), teachers (see Section 4), neighbors and the broader community a child is embedded in (see Section 5), one's cultural group (see Section 6), as well as therapists and counselors (see Section 7). However, the links among the child, the caregiver, and even the larger community are bidirectional and dynamic (Masten, 2018; Ungar & Theron, 2020). For example, supportive parenting can promote the development of social skills, which in turn might help the child secure social and emotional support from additional sources, such as teachers or peers. A parent's ability to provide support may also depend on the characteristics of the child, like their personality, and on the broader community and culture they are immersed in (Alen et al., 2024; Masten, 2018). As such, bolstering children's chances of displaying resilience requires investment from everyone across all layers of society. If we can provide multiple sources of support, teach coping and problem-solving skills, and provide numerous opportunities for children to participate in safe and enriching activities, we can ensure that children will thrive and show resilience when facing life's inevitable challenges.

References

Aafjes-van Doorn, K., Kamsteeg, C., & Silberschatz, G. (2020). Cognitive mediators of the relationship between adverse childhood experiences and adult psychopathology: A systematic review. *Development and Psychopathology*, *32*(3), 1017–1029. https://doi.org/10.1017/S0954579419001317.

Adam, E. K., Hittner, E. F., Thomas, S. E., Villaume, S. C., & Nwafor, E. E. (2020). Racial discrimination and ethnic racial identity in adolescence as modulators of HPA axis activity. *Development and Psychopathology*, *32*(5), 1669–1684. https://doi.org/10.1017/S095457942000111X.

Adams, R., Bishop, S., & Taylor, J. L. (2020). Peer victimization. In F. R. Volkmar (Ed.), *Encyclopedia of Autism Spectrum Disorders* (pp. 1–8). Springer New York. https://doi.org/10.1007/978-1-4614-6435-8_102151-2.

Adams, R. E., Santo, J. B., & Bukowski, W. M. (2011). The presence of a best friend buffers the effects of negative experiences. *Developmental Psychology*, *47*(6), 1786–1791. https://doi.org/10.1037/a0025401.

Afifi, T. O., & MacMillan, H. L. (2011). Resilience following Child Maltreatment: A Review of Protective Factors. *The Canadian Journal of Psychiatry*, *56*(5), 266–272. https://doi.org/10.1177/070674371105600505.

Agrawal, A., Garg, R., & Urajnik, D. (2010). Appraisal of school-based stressors by fourth-grade children: A mixed method approach. *Creative Education*, *01*(03), Article 03. https://doi.org/10.4236/ce.2010.13029.

Ahnert, L., Harwardt-Heinecke, E., Kappler, G., Eckstein-Madry, T., & Milatz, A. (2012). Student–teacher relationships and classroom climate in first grade: How do they relate to students' stress regulation? *Attachment & Human Development*, *14*(3), 249–263. https://doi.org/10.1080/14616734.2012.673277.

Aisenberg, E., & Herrenkohl, T. (2008). Community violence in context: Risk and resilience in children and families. *Journal of Interpersonal Violence*, *23*(3), 296–315. https://doi.org/10.1177/0886260507312287.

Aiyer, S. M., Zimmerman, M. A., Morrel-Samuels, S., & Reischl, T. M. (2015). From broken windows to busy streets: A community empowerment perspective. *Health Education & Behavior*, *42*(2), 137–147. https://doi.org/10.1177/1090198114558590.

Alen, N. V., Deer, L. K., Karimi, M., et al. (2021). Children's altruism following acute stress: The role of autonomic nervous system activity and social support. *Developmental Science*, *24*(5), e13099. https://doi.org/10.1111/desc.13099.

References

Alen, N. V., Hostinar, C. E., & Luthar, S. S. (2024). Promoting resilience of children, parents, and families in the service of health promotion. In Bornstein, Marc H. and Shah, Prachi E. (Eds.), *APA Handbook of Pediatric Psychology, Developmental Behavioral Pediatrics, and Developmental Science* (pp. 325–344). American Psychological Association.

Alen, N. V., Shields, G. S., Nemer, A., et al. (2022). A systematic review and meta-analysis of the association between parenting and child autonomic nervous system activity. *Neuroscience and Biobehavioral Reviews, 139*, 104734. https://doi.org/10.1016/j.neubiorev.2022.104734.

Alen, N. V., Sloan, R. P., Seeman, T. E., & Hostinar, C. E. (2020). Childhood parental warmth and heart rate variability in midlife: Implications for health. *Personal Relationships, 27*(3), 506–525. https://doi.org/10.1111/pere.12329.

American Psychological Association (2018). *Dictionary of Psychology*. Retrieved August 15, 2024, https://dictionary.apa.org/psychological-distress.

Andrews, K., Dunn, J. R., Prime, H., et al. (2021). Effects of household chaos and parental responsiveness on child executive functions: A novel, multi-method approach. *BMC Psychology, 9*, 147. https://doi.org/10.1186/s40359-021-00651-1.

Apter-Levi, Y., Pratt, M., Vakart, A., et al. (2016). Maternal depression across the first years of life compromises child psychosocial adjustment; relations to child HPA-axis functioning. *Psychoneuroendocrinology, 64*, 47–56. https://doi.org/10.1016/j.psyneuen.2015.11.006.

Arens, A. K., & Morin, A. J. S. (2016). Relations between teachers' emotional exhaustion and students' educational outcomes. *Journal of Educational Psychology, 108*(6), 800–813. https://doi.org/10.1037/edu0000105.

Argabright, S. T., Moore, T. M., Visoki, E., DiDomenico, G. E., Taylor, J. H., & Barzilay, R. (2022). Association between racial/ethnic discrimination and pubertal development in early adolescence. *Psychoneuroendocrinology, 140*, 105727. https://doi.org/10.1016/j.psyneuen.2022.105727.

Armitage, R. (2021). Bullying in children: Impact on child health. *BMJ Paediatrics Open, 5*(1), e000939. https://doi.org/10.1136/bmjpo-2020-000939.

Arvidson, J., Kinniburgh, K., Howard, K., et al. (2011). Treatment of complex trauma in young children: Developmental and cultural considerations in application of the ARC intervention model. *Journal of Child & Adolescent Trauma, 4*(1), 34–51. https://doi.org/10.1080/19361521.2011.545046.

August, G. J., Realmuto, G. M., Hektner, J. M., & Bloomquist, M. L. (2001). An integrated components preventive intervention for aggressive elementary school children: The early risers program. *Journal of Consulting and Clinical Psychology, 69*(4), 614–626. https://doi.org/10.1037/0022-006X.69.4.614.

Austin, J. L., Jeffries, E. F., Winston, W., & Brady, S. S. (2022). Race-related stressors and resources for resilience: Associations with emotional health, conduct problems, and academic investment among African American early adolescents. *Journal of the American Academy of Child & Adolescent Psychiatry, 61*(4), 544–553. https://doi.org/10.1016/j.jaac.2021.05.020.

Badanes, L. S., Watamura, S. E., & Hankin, B. L. (2011). Hypocortisolism as a potential marker of allostatic load in children: Associations with family risk and internalizing disorders. *Development and Psychopathology, 23*(3), 881–896. https://doi.org/10.1017/S095457941100037X.

Bates, C. R., Nicholson, L. M., Rea, E. M., Hagy, H. A., & Bohnert, A. M. (2021). Life interrupted: Family routines buffer stress during the COVID-19 pandemic. *Journal of Child and Family Studies, 30*(11), 2641–2651. https://doi.org/10.1007/s10826-021-02063-6.

Bateson, G. (1972). Steps to an ecology of mind. New York: Ballantine.

Bathory, E., & Tomopoulos, S. (2017). Sleep regulation, physiology and development, sleep duration and patterns, and sleep hygiene in infants, toddlers, and preschool-age children. *Current Problems in Pediatric and Adolescent Health Care, 47*(2), 29–42. https://doi.org/10.1016/j.cppeds.2016.12.001.

Baumrind, D. (1971). Current patterns of parental authority. *Developmental Psychology, 4*(1, Pt.2), 1–103. https://doi.org/10.1037/h0030372.

Behnsen, P., Buil, M., Koot, S., Huizink, A., & van Lier, P. (2018). Classroom social experiences in early elementary school relate to diurnal cortisol levels. *Psychoneuroendocrinology, 87*, 1–8. https://doi.org/10.1016/j.psyneuen.2017.09.025.

Bell, M. A. (2020). Mother-child behavioral and physiological synchrony. In Benson, Janette B. (Ed.), *Advances in Child Development and Behavior* (Vol. 58, pp. 163–188). Elsevier. https://doi.org/10.1016/bs.acdb.2020.01.006.

Benner, A. D., & Graham, S. (2013). The antecedents and consequences of racial/ethnic discrimination during adolescence: Does the source of discrimination matter? *Developmental Psychology, 49*(8), 1602–1613. https://doi.org/10.1037/a0030557.

Bennett, A. C., Brewer, K. C., & Rankin, K. M. (2012). The association of child mental health conditions and parent mental health status among U.S. children, 2007. *Maternal and Child Health Journal, 16*(6), 1266–1275. https://doi.org/10.1007/s10995-011-0888-4.

Bernard, K., Hostinar, C. E., & Dozier, M. (2019). Longitudinal associations between attachment quality in infancy, C-reactive protein in early childhood, and BMI in middle childhood: Preliminary evidence from a CPS-referred sample. *Attachment & Human Development, 21*(1), 5–22. https://doi.org/10.1080/14616734.2018.1541513.

Bernard, K., Meade, E., & Dozier, M. (2013). Parental synchrony and nurturance as targets in an attachment based intervention: Building upon mary ainsworth's insights about mother-infant interaction. *Attachment & Human Development*, *15*(5–6), 507–523. https://doi.org/10.1080/14616734.2013.820920.

Bethell, C. D., Newacheck, P., Hawes, E., & Halfon, N. (2014). Adverse childhood experiences: Assessing the impact on health and school engagement and the mitigating role of resilience. *Health Affairs (Project Hope)*, *33*(12), 2106–2115. https://doi.org/10.1377/hlthaff.2014.0914.

Blair, C. (2010). Stress and the development of self-regulation in context: Stress and the development of self-regulation. *Child Development Perspectives*, *4*(3), 181–188. https://doi.org/10.1111/j.1750-8606.2010.00145.x.

Blair, C., & Raver, C. C. (2012). Child development in the context of adversity: Experiential canalization of brain and behavior. *The American Psychologist*, *67*(4), 309–318. https://doi.org/10.1037/a0027493.

Bolger, K. E., & Patterson, C. J. (2003). Sequelae of child maltreatment: Vulnerability and resilience. In S. S. Luthar (Ed.), *Resilience and Vulnerability: Adaptation in the Context of Childhood Adversities* (pp. 156–181). Cambridge University Press. https://doi.org/10.1017/CBO9780511615788.009.

Borelli, J. L., Burkhart, M. L., Rasmussen, H. F., Smiley, P. A., & Hellemann, G. (2018). Children's and mothers' cardiovascular reactivity to a standardized laboratory stressor: Unique relations with maternal anxiety and overcontrol. Emotion, *18*(3), 369–385. https://doi.org/10.1037/emo0000320.

Borelli, J. L., Gaskin, G., Smiley, P., et al. (2023). Multisystem physiological reactivity during help-seeking for attachment needs in school-aged children: Differences as a function of attachment. *Attachment & Human Development*, *25*(1), 117–131. https://doi.org/10.1080/14616734.2021.1913874.

Bornstein, M. H. (2012). Cultural approaches to parenting. *Parenting*, *12*(2–3), 212–221. https://doi.org/10.1080/15295192.2012.683359.

Bowen Center for the Study of the Family (2024). *Introduction to the Eight Concepts*. May 6, 2024, www.thebowencenter.org/introduction-eight-concepts.

Bowlby, J. (1969). *Attachment and Loss. 1*: *Attachment* (2nd ed., Vol. 1). Basic Books.

Braddock, A. S., Phad, A., Tabak, R., et al. (2021). Assessing racial and ethnic discrimination in children: A scoping review of available measures for child health disparities research. *Health Equity*, *5*(1), 727–737. https://doi.org/10.1089/heq.2021.0008.

Brewin, C. R., Cloitre, M., Hyland, P., et al. (2017). A review of current evidence regarding the ICD-11 proposals for diagnosing PTSD and complex PTSD. *Clinical Psychology Review, 58,* 1–15. https://doi.org/10.1016/j.cpr.2017.09.001.

Brody, G. H., Chen, Y., Murry, V. M., et al. (2006). Perceived discrimination and the adjustment of African American youths: A five-year longitudinal analysis with contextual moderation effects. *Child Development, 77*(5), 1170–1189. https://doi.org/10.1111/j.1467-8624.2006.00927.x.

Brosschot, J. F., Verkuil, B., & Thayer, J. F. (2017). Exposed to events that never happen: Generalized unsafety, the default stress response, and prolonged autonomic activity. *Neuroscience and biobehavioral reviews, 74*(Pt B), 287–296. https://doi.org/10.1016/j.neubiorev.2016.07.019.

Broyles, S. T., Staiano, A. E., Drazba, K. T., et al. (2012). Elevated C-reactive protein in children from risky neighborhoods: Evidence for a stress pathway linking neighborhoods and inflammation in children. *PLoS ONE, 7*(9), e45419. https://doi.org/10.1371/journal.pone.0045419.

Buettner, C. K., Jeon, L., Hur, E., & Garcia, R. E. (2016). Teachers' social–emotional capacity: Factors associated with teachers' responsiveness and professional commitment. *Early Education and Development, 27*(7), 1018–1039. https://doi.org/10.1080/10409289.2016.1168227.

Buhler-Wassmann, A. C., Hibel, L. C., Fondren, K., & Valentino, K. (2021). Child diurnal cortisol differs based on profiles of maternal emotion socialization in high risk, low income, and racially diverse families. *Developmental Psychobiology, 63*(3), 538–555. https://doi.org/10.1002/dev.22048.

Bunea, I., Szentágotai-Tătar, A. & Miu, A. C. (2017). Early-life adversity and cortisol response to social stress: A meta-analysis. *Translational Psychiatry, 7,* 1274. https://doi.org/10.1038/s41398-017-0032-3.

Burdette, H. L., & Whitaker, R. C. (2005). Resurrecting free play in young children: Looking beyond fitness and fatness to attention, affiliation, and affect. *Archives of Pediatrics & Adolescent Medicine, 159*(1), 46. https://doi.org/10.1001/archpedi.159.1.46.

Burke Harris, N. (2018). *The Deepest Well: Healing the Long-Term Effects of Childhood Adversity.* Houghton Mifflin Harcourt.

Burke, N. J., Hellman, J. L., Scott, B. G., Weems, C. F., & Carrion, V. G. (2011). The impact of adverse childhood experiences on an urban pediatric population. *Child Abuse & Neglect, 35*(6), 408–413. https://doi.org/10.1016/j.chiabu.2011.02.006.

Burlew, A. K., Peteet, B. J., McCuistian, C., & Miller-Roenigk, B. D. (2019). Best practices for researching diverse groups. *American Journal of Orthopsychiatry, 89*(3), 354–368. https://doi.org/10.1037/ort0000350.

Byrne, M. L., Badcock, P. B., Simmons, J. G., et al. (2017). Self-reported parenting style is associated with children's inflammation and immune activation. *Journal of Family Psychology*, *31*(3), 374–380. https://doi.org/10.1037/fam0000254.

Cafaro, C. L., Gonzalez Molina, E., Patton, E., McMahon, S. D., & Brown, M. (2023). Meta-analyses of teacher-delivered trauma-based and trauma-informed care interventions. *Psychological Trauma: Theory, Research, Practice, and Policy*, *15*(7), 1177–1187. https://doi.org/10.1037/tra0001515.

California Evidence-Based Clearinghouse for Child Welfare (2025). Program registry. Retrieved May 31, 2025, www.cebc4cw.org/registry/.

Callaghan, B. L., Fields, A., Gee, D. G., et al. (2019). Mind and gut: Associations between mood and gastrointestinal distress in children exposed to adversity. *Development and Psychopathology*, 1–20. https://doi.org/10.1017/S0954579419000087.

Cannon, W. B. (1915). *Bodily Changes in Pain, Hunger, Fear and Rage*. D. Appleton.

Carro, N., Ibar, C., D'Adamo, P., et al. (2023). Hair cortisol reduction and social integration enhancement after a mindfulness-based intervention in children. *Child: Care, Health and Development*, *49*(1), 73–79. https://doi.org/10.1111/cch.13008.

Carter, J. R., & Goldstein, D. S. (2015). Sympathoneural and adrenomedullary responses to mental stress. *Comprehensive Physiology*, *5*(1), 119–146. https://doi.org/10.1002/cphy.c140030.

Causadias, J. M., Vitriol, J. A., & Atkin, A. L. (2018). Do we overemphasize the role of culture in the behavior of racial/ethnic minorities? Evidence of a cultural (mis)attribution bias in American psychology. *American Psychologist*, *73*(3), 243–255.

Cecil-Karb, R., & Grogan-Kaylor, A. (2009). Childhood body mass index in community context: Neighborhood safety, television viewing, and growth trajectories of BMI. *Health & Social Work*, *34*(3), 169–177. https://doi.org/10.1093/hsw/34.3.169.

Center on the Developing Child (2024). Toxic stress. Retrieved August 15, 2024, https://developingchild.harvard.edu/science/key-concepts/toxic-stress/.

Chen, E., Hayen, R., Le, V., et al. (2019). Neighborhood social conditions, family relationships, and childhood asthma. *Pediatrics*, *144*(2), e20183300. https://doi.org/10.1542/peds.2018-3300.

Chen, E., Lam, P. H., Yu, T., & Brody, G. H. (2023). Racial disparities in school belonging and prospective associations with diabetes and metabolic syndrome. *JAMA Pediatrics*, *177*(2), 141–148.

Cheng, Z., Su, J., Zhang, K., Jiang, H., & Li, B. (2022). Epigenetic mechanism of early life stress-induced depression: Focus on the neurotransmitter systems. *Frontiers in Cell and Developmental Biology*, *10*, 1–13. https://doi.org/10.3389/fcell.2022.929732.

Children's Defense Fund (2023). *2023 State of America's Children Report. Child Population*. Retrieved May 31, 2025, www.childrensdefense.org/tools-and-resources/the-state-of-americas-children/soac-child-population/.

Cicchetti, D. (2013). Annual research review: Resilient functioning in maltreated children – past, present, and future perspectives: Resilient functioning in maltreated children. *Journal of Child Psychology and Psychiatry*, *54*(4), 402–422. https://doi.org/10.1111/j.1469-7610.2012.02608.x.

Cicchetti, D., & Blender, J. A. (2006). A multiple-levels-of-analysis perspective on resilience: Implications for the developing brain, neural plasticity, and preventive interventions. *Annals of the New York Academy of Sciences*, *1094*(1), 248–258. https://doi.org/10.1196/annals.1376.029.

Cicchetti, D., & Toth, S. L. (2005). Child maltreatment. *Annual Review of Clinical Psychology*, *1*(Volume 1, 2005), 409–438. https://doi.org/10.1146/annurev.clinpsy.1.102803.144029.

Ciula, R., & Skinner, C. (2015). Income and beyond: Taking the measure of child deprivation in the United States. *Child Indicators Research*, *8*(3), 491–515. https://doi.org/10.1007/s12187-014-9246-6.

Cohen, J. A., Mannarino, A. P., & Deblinger, E. (2006). *Treating Trauma and Traumatic Grief in Children and Adolescents* (pp. xvi, 256). Guilford Press.

Cohodes, E. M., McCauley, S., & Gee, D. G. (2021). Parental buffering of stress in the time of COVID-19: Family-level factors may moderate the association between pandemic-related stress and youth symptomatology. *Research on Child and Adolescent Psychopathology*, *49*(7), 935–948. https://doi.org/10.1007/s10802-020-00732-6.

Cohodes, E. M., Sisk, L. M., Keding, T. J., et al. (2023). Characterizing experiential elements of early-life stress to inform resilience: Buffering effects of controllability and predictability and the importance of their timing. *Development and Psychopathology*, *35*(5), 2288–2301. https://doi.org/10.1017/S0954579423000822.

Cole, P. M., Martin, S. E., & Dennis, T. A. (2004). Emotion regulation as a scientific construct: Methodological challenges and directions for child development research. *Child Development*, *75*(2), 317–333. https://doi.org/10.1111/j.1467-8624.2004.00673.x.

Coley, R. L., Lynch, A. D., & Kull, M. (2015). Early exposure to environmental chaos and children's physical and mental health. *Early Childhood Research Quarterly*, *32*, 94–104. https://doi.org/10.1016/j.ecresq.2015.03.001.

Compas, B. E. (1987). Stress and life events during childhood and adolescence. *Clinical Psychology Review*, *7*(3), 275–302. https://doi.org/10.1016/0272-7358(87)90037-7.

Conger, R. D., Conger, K. J., Elder, G. H., et al. (1992). A family process model of economic hardship and adjustment of early adolescent boys. *Child Development*, *63*(3), 526–541. https://doi.org/10.2307/1131344.

Conrey, S. C., Burrell, A. R., Brokamp, C., et al. (2022). Comparison of neighborhood deprivation index and food desert status as environmental predictors of early childhood obesity. *International Public Health Journal*, *14*(3), 263–276.

Copeland, W. E., Wolke, D., Lereya, S. T., et al. (2014). Childhood bullying involvement predicts low-grade systemic inflammation into adulthood. *Proceedings of the National Academy of Sciences*, *111*(21), 7570–7575. https://doi.org/10.1073/pnas.1323641111.

Cowen, P. S. (2001). Effectiveness of a parent education intervention for at-risk families. *Journal for Specialists in Pediatric Nursing*, *6*(2), 73–82. https://doi.org/10.1111/j.1744-6155.2001.tb00124.x.

Crowe, J., Lacy, C., & Columbus, Y. (2018). Barriers to food security and community stress in an urban food desert. *Urban Science*, *2*(2), 46. https://doi.org/10.3390/urbansci2020046.

Crusto, C. A., Whitson, M. L., Walling, S. M., et al. (2010). Posttraumatic stress among young urban children exposed to family violence and other potentially traumatic events. *Journal of Traumatic Stress*, *23*(6), 716–724. https://doi.org/10.1002/jts.20590.

Daníelsdóttir, S., & Ingudóttir, J. (2020). *The First 1000 Days in the Nordic Countries: A Situation Analysis*. Nordic Council of Ministers. https://doi.org/10.6027/nord2020-051.

Davies, P. T., Cummings, E. M., & Winter, M. A. (2004). Pathways between profiles of family functioning, child security in the interparental subsystem, and child psychological problems. *Development and Psychopathology*, *16*(3), 525–550. https://doi.org/10.1017/S0954579404004651.

Davis, C., & Turner-Cobb, J. M. (2023). The perceived stress scale for kids (PeSSKi): Initial development of a brief measure for children aged 7–11 years. *Stress and Health*, *39*(1), 125–136. https://doi.org/10.1002/smi.3174.

Davis, E. P., & Glynn, L. M. (2024). Annual Research Review: The power of predictability – patterns of signals in early life shape neurodevelopment and mental health trajectories. *Journal of Child Psychology and Psychiatry*, *65*(4), 508–534. https://doi.org/10.1111/jcpp.13958.

Deater-Deckard, K., Lansford, J. E., Malone, P. S., et al. (2011). The association between parental warmth and control in thirteen cultural groups. *Journal of Family Psychology, 25*(5), 790–794. https://doi.org/10.1037/a0025120.

DePasquale, C. E. (2020). A systematic review of caregiver–child physiological synchrony across systems: Associations with behavior and child functioning. *Development and Psychopathology, 32*(5), 1754–1777. https://doi.org/10.1017/S0954579420001236.

Dettling, A. C., Gunnar, M. R., & Donzella, B. (1999). Cortisol levels of young children in full-day childcare centers: Relations with age and temperament. *Psychoneuroendocrinology, 24*(5), 519–536. https://doi.org/10.1016/S0306-4530(99)00009-8.

Dodge, K. A., Goodman, W. B., Murphy, R., O'Donnell, K., & Sato, J. (2013). Toward population impact from home visiting. *Zero to Three, 33*(3), 17–23.

Doom, J. R., Cook, S. H., Sturza, J., et al. (2018). Family conflict, chaos, and negative life events predict cortisol activity in low-income children. *Developmental Psychobiology, 60*(4), 364–379. https://doi.org/10.1002/dev.21602.

Doom, J. R., Vanzomeren-Dohm, A. A., & Simpson, J. A. (2016). Early unpredictability predicts increased adolescent externalizing behaviors and substance use: A life history perspective. *Development and Psychopathology, 28*(4 Pt 2), 1505–1516. https://doi.org/10.1017/S0954579415001169.

Doretto, V., & Scivoletto, S. (2018). Effects of early neglect experience on recognition and processing of facial expressions: A systematic review. *Brain Sciences, 8*(1), Article 1. https://doi.org/10.3390/brainsci8010010.

Dowdney, L. (2000). Childhood bereavement following parental death. *Journal of Child Psychology and Psychiatry, 41*(7), 819–830. https://doi.org/10.1111/1469-7610.00670.

Doyle, C., & Cicchetti, D. (2017). From the cradle to the grave: The effect of adverse caregiving environments on attachment and relationships throughout the lifespan. *Clinical Psychology: Science and Practice, 24*(2), 203–217. https://doi.org/10.1111/cpsp.12192.

Dozier, M., Lindhiem, O., Lewis, E., et al. (2009). Effects of a foster parent training program on young children's attachment behaviors: Preliminary evidence from a randomized clinical trial. *Child and Adolescent Social Work Journal, 26*(4), 321–332. https://doi.org/10.1007/s10560-009-0165-1.

Dozier, M., Peloso, E., Lindhiem, O., et al.(2006). Developing evidence-based interventions for foster children: An example of a randomized clinical trial with infants and toddlers. *Journal of Social Issues, 62*(4), 767–785. https://doi.org/10.1111/j.1540-4560.2006.00486.x.

Drake, B., & Rank, M. R. (2009). The racial divide among American children in poverty: Reassessing the importance of neighborhood. *Children and Youth Services Review*, *31*(12), 1264-1271.

Dubow, E. F., & Tisak, J. (1989). The relation between stressful life events and adjustment in elementary school children: The role of social support and social problem-solving skills. *Child Development*, *60*(6), 1412–1423. https://doi.org/10.2307/1130931.

Dubowitz, H., Feigelman, S., Lane, W., & Kim, J. (2009). Pediatric primary care to help prevent child maltreatment: The safe environment for every kid (SEEK) model. *Pediatrics*, *123*(3), 858–864. https://doi.org/10.1542/peds.2008-1376.

Duncan, G. J., Brooks-Gunn, J., & Klebanov, P. K. (1994). Economic deprivation and early childhood development. *Child Development*, *65*(2), 296–318. https://doi.org/10.2307/1131385.

Dunning, D., Tudor, K., Radley, L., et al. (2022). Do mindfulness-based programmes improve the cognitive skills, behaviour and mental health of children and adolescents? An updated meta-analysis of randomised controlled trials. *BMJ Ment Health*, *25*(3), 135–142. https://doi.org/10.1136/ebmental-2022-300464.

Dvir, Y., Ford, J. D., Hill, M., & Frazier, J. A. (2014). Childhood maltreatment, emotional dysregulation, and psychiatric comorbidities. *Harvard Review of Psychiatry*, *22*(3), 149. https://doi.org/10.1097/HRP.0000000000000014.

Eisenberg, N. (2020). Findings, issues, and new directions for research on emotion socialization. *Developmental Psychology*, *56*(3), 664–670. https://doi.org/10.1037/dev0000906.

Eisenberg, N., Cumberland, A., & Spinrad, T. L. (1998). Parental socialization of emotion. *Psychological Inquiry*, *9*(4), 241–273. https://doi.org/10.1207/s15327965pli0904_1.

Elledge, L. C., Elledge, A. R., Newgent, R. A., & Cavell, T. A. (2016). Social risk and peer victimization in elementary school children: The protective role of teacher-student relationships. *Journal of Abnormal Child Psychology*, *44*(4), 691–703. https://doi.org/10.1007/s10802-015-0074-z.

Ellis, B. J., Figueredo, A. J., Brumbach, B. H., & Schlomer, G. L. (2009). Fundamental dimensions of environmental risk. *Human Nature*, *20*(2), 204–268. https://doi.org/10.1007/s12110-009-9063-7.

England-Mason, G., & Gonzalez, A. (2020). Intervening to shape children's emotion regulation: A review of emotion socialization parenting programs for young children. *Emotion*, *20*(1), 98–104. https://doi.org/10.1037/emo0000638.

Espelage, D. L., Hong, J. S., Rao, M. A., & Thornberg, R. (2015). Understanding ecological factors associated with bullying across the elementary to middle school transition in the United States. *Violence and Victims*, *30*(3), 470–487. https://doi.org/10.1891/0886-6708.vv-d-14-00046.

Evans, G. W. (2004). The Environment of Childhood Poverty. *American Psychologist*, *59*(2), 77–92. https://doi.org/10.1037/0003-066X.59.2.77

Fang, R., Zhang, R., Hosseini, E., et al. (2022). Prevent over-fitting and redundancy in physiological signal analyses for stress detection. *2022 IEEE International Conference on Bioinformatics and Biomedicine (BIBM)*, 2585–2588. https://doi.org/10.1109/BIBM55620.2022.9995121.

Feldman, R. (2007). Parent-infant synchrony and the construction of shared timing; physiological precursors, developmental outcomes, and risk conditions. *Journal of Child Psychology and Psychiatry, and Allied Disciplines*, *48*(3–4), 329–354. https://doi.org/10.1111/j.1469-7610.2006.01701.x.

Felitti, V. J., Anda, R. F., Nordenberg, D., et al. (1998). Relationship of childhood abuse and household dysfunction to many of the leading causes of death in adults. *American Journal of Preventive Medicine*, *14*(4), 245–258. https://doi.org/10.1016/S0749-3797(98)00017-8.

Ferguson, C. J. (2013). Spanking, corporal punishment and negative long-term outcomes: A meta-analytic review of longitudinal studies. *Clinical Psychology Review*, *33*(1), 196–208. https://doi.org/10.1016/j.cpr.2012.11.002.

Fisher, A. V., Godwin, K. E., & Seltman, H. (2014). Visual environment, attention allocation, and learning in young children: When too much of a good thing may be bad. *Psychological Science*, *25*(7), 1362–1370. https://doi.org/10.1177/0956797614533801.

Fleckman, J. M., Tokarz, S., Claire Craig-Kuhn, M., Wallace, M. E., & Theall, K. P. (2022). Neighborhood matters: Neighborhood violence, collective efficacy, and social emotional development in early childhood. *Children and Youth Services Review*, *143*, 106700. https://doi.org/10.1016/j.childyouth.2022.106700.

Fraguas, D., Díaz-Caneja, C. M., Ayora, M., et al. (2021). Assessment of school anti-bullying interventions: A meta-analysis of randomized clinical trials. *JAMA Pediatrics*, *175*(1), 44. https://doi.org/10.1001/jamapediatrics.2020.3541.

Freiberg, H. J. (2005). *School Climate: Measuring, Improving, and Sustaining Healthy Learning Environments*. Routledge.

Fremont, W. P. (2003). School refusal in children and adolescents. *American Family Physician*, *68*(8), 1555–1561.

Fries, E., Hesse, J., Hellhammer, J., & Hellhammer, D. H. (2005). A new view on hypocortisolism. *Psychoneuroendocrinology*, *30*(10), 1010–1016. https://doi.org/10.1016/j.psyneuen.2005.04.006.

Galán, C. A., Shaw, D. S., Dishion, T. J., & Wilson, M. N. (2017). Neighborhood deprivation during early childhood and conduct problems in middle childhood: Mediation by aggressive response generation. *Journal of Abnormal Child Psychology*, *45*(5), 935–946. https://doi.org/10.1007/s10802-016-0209-x.

Garmezy, N. (1971). Vulnerability research and the issue of primary prevention. *The American Journal of Orthopsychiatry*, *41*(1), 101–116. https://doi.org/10.1111/j.1939-0025.1971.tb01111.x.

Gaylord-Harden, N. K., Burrow, A. L., & Cunningham, J. A. (2012). A cultural-asset framework for investigating successful adaptation to stress in African American youth. *Child Development Perspectives*, *6*(3), 264–271. https://doi.org/10.1111/j.1750-8606.2012.00236.x.

Gilgoff, R., Mengelkoch, S., Elbers, J., et al. (2024). The stress phenotyping framework: A multidisciplinary biobehavioral approach for assessing and therapeutically targeting maladaptive stress physiology. *Stress*, *27*(1), 2327333. https://doi.org/10.1080/10253890.2024.2327333.

Gilliam, W. S., Maupin, A. N., & Reyes, C. R. (2016). Early childhood mental health consultation: Results of a statewide random-controlled evaluation. *Journal of the American Academy of Child & Adolescent Psychiatry*, *55*(9), 754–761. https://doi.org/10.1016/j.jaac.2016.06.006.

Ginwright, S. (2021, January 19). *The Future of Healing*: Shifting From Trauma-Informed Care to Healing-Centered Engagement – Youth Research and Evaluation eXchange. https://youthrex.com/blog/the-future-of-healing-shifting-from-trauma-informed-care-to-healing-centered-engagement/.

Gleason, T. R., Tarsha, M. S., Kurth, A. M., & Narvaez, D. (2021). Opportunities for free play and young children's autonomic regulation. *Developmental Psychobiology*, *63*(6), e22134. https://doi.org/10.1002/dev.22134.

Glynn, L. M., Davis, E. P., Luby, J. L., Baram, T. Z., & Sandman, C. A. (2021). A predictable home environment may protect child mental health during the COVID-19 pandemic. *Neurobiology of Stress*, *14*, 100291. https://doi.org/10.1016/j.ynstr.2020.100291.

González Ramírez, M. L., García Vázquez, J. P., Rodríguez, M. D., et al. (2023). Wearables for stress management: A scoping review. *Healthcare (Basel, Switzerland)*, *11*(17), 2369. https://doi.org/10.3390/healthcare11172369.

Goodman, W. B., Dodge, K. A., Bai, Y., Murphy, R. A., & O'Donnell, K. (2021). Effect of a universal postpartum nurse home visiting program on child maltreatment and emergency medical care at 5 years of age: A randomized clinical trial. *JAMA Network Open*, *4*(7), e2116024. https://doi.org/10.1001/jamanetworkopen.2021.16024.

Granic, I., & Patterson, G. R. (2006). Toward a comprehensive model of antisocial development: A dynamic systems approach. *Psychological Review*, *113*(1), 101–131. https://doi.org/10.1037/0033-295X.113.1.101.

Grasso, D., Boonsiri, J., Lipschitz, D., et al. (2009). Posttraumatic stress disorder: The missed diagnosis. *Child Welfare*, *88*(4), 157–176.

Greenberg, M. T., Kusche, C. A., Cook, E. T., & Quamma, J. P. (1995). Promoting emotional competence in school-aged children: The effects of the PATHS curriculum. *Development and Psychopathology*, *7*(1), 117–136. https://doi.org/10.1017/S0954579400006374.

Groeneveld, M. G., Vermeer, H. J., Linting, M., et al. (2013). Children's hair cortisol as a biomarker of stress at school entry. *Stress*, *16*(6), 711–715. https://doi.org/10.3109/10253890.2013.817553.

Gross, D., Garvey, C., Julion, W., et al. (2009). Efficacy of the Chicago parent program with low-income African American and Latino parents of young children. *Prevention Science*, *10*(1), 54–65. https://doi.org/10.1007/s11121-008-0116-7.

Gruenewald, T. L., Karlamangla, A. S., Hu, P., et al. (2012). History of socioeconomic disadvantage and allostatic load in later life. *Social Science & Medicine (1982)*, *74*(1), 75–83. https://doi.org/10.1016/j.socscimed.2011.09.037.

Grusec, J. E. (2011). Socialization processes in the family: Social and emotional development. *Annual Review of Psychology*, *62*(1), 243–269. https://doi.org/10.1146/annurev.psych.121208.131650.

Gunnar, M. R. (2000). Early adversity and the development of stress reactivity and regulation. In Charles A. Nelson (Ed.), *The Effects of Early Adversity on Neurobehavioral Development* (163–200). Psychology Press.

Gunnar, M. R. (2021). Forty years of research on stress and development: What have we learned and future directions. *The American Psychologist*, *76*(9), 1372–1384. https://doi.org/10.1037/amp0000893.

Gunnar, M. R., Brodersen, L., Nachmias, M., Buss, K., & Rigatuso, J. (1996). Stress reactivity and attachment security. *Developmental Psychobiology*, *29*(3), 191–204. https://doi.org/10.1002/(SICI)1098-2302(199604)29:3<191::AID-DEV1>3.0.CO;2-M.

Gunnar, M. R., DePasquale, C. E., Reid, B. M., Donzella, B., & Miller, B. S. (2019). Pubertal stress recalibration reverses the effects of early life stress in postinstitutionalized children. *Proceedings of the National Academy of Sciences*, *116*(48), 23984–23988. https://doi.org/10.1073/pnas.1909699116.

Gunnar, M. R., & Donzella, B. (2002). Social regulation of the cortisol levels in early human development. *Psychoneuroendocrinology, 27*(1–2), 199–220. https://doi.org/10.1016/s0306-4530(01)00045-2.

Gunnar, M. R., Doom, J. R., & Esposito, E. A. (2015). Psychoneuroendocrinology of Stress. In M. E. Lamb & R. M. Lerner (Eds.), *Handbook of Child Psychology and Developmental Science* (pp. 1–46). John Wiley & Sons. https://doi.org/10.1002/9781118963418.childpsy304.

Gunnar, M. R., Sebanc, A. M., Tout, K., Donzella, B., & van Dulmen, M. M. H. (2003). Peer rejection, temperament, and cortisol activity in preschoolers. *Developmental Psychobiology, 43*(4), 346–368. https://doi.org/10.1002/dev.10144.

Gunnar, M. R., Talge, N. M., & Herrera, A. (2009). Stressor paradigms in developmental studies: What does and does not work to produce mean increases in salivary cortisol. *Psychoneuroendocrinology, 34*(7), 953–967. https://doi.org/10.1016/j.psyneuen.2009.02.010.

Gunnar, M. R., & Vazquez, D. M. (2001). Low cortisol and a flattening of expected daytime rhythm: Potential indices of risk in human development. *Development and Psychopathology, 13*(3), 515–538. https://doi.org/10.1017/S0954579401003066.

Gutteling, B. M., Weerth, C. de, & Buitelaar, J. K. (2005). Prenatal stress and children's cortisol reaction to the first day of school. *Psychoneuroendocrinology, 30*(6), 541–549. https://doi.org/10.1016/j.psyneuen.2005.01.002.

Hakman, M., Chaffin, M., Funderburk, B., & Silovsky, J. F. (2009). Change trajectories for parent-child interaction sequences during parent-child interaction therapy for child physical abuse. *Child Abuse & Neglect, 33*(7), 461–470. https://doi.org/10.1016/j.chiabu.2008.08.003.

Hall, J., & Lindorff, A. (2017). Children's transition to school: Relationships between preschool attendance, cortisol patterns, and effortful control. *The Educational and Developmental Psychologist, 34*(1), 1–18. https://doi.org/10.1017/edp.2017.3.

Hamre, B. K., & Pianta, R. C. (2001). Early teacher–child relationships and the trajectory of children's school outcomes through eighth grade. *Child Development, 72*(2), 625–638. https://doi.org/10.1111/1467-8624.00301.

Hang, S., Jost, G. M., Guyer, A. E., et al. (2024). Understanding the development of chronic loneliness in youth. *Child Development Perspectives, 18*(1), 44–53. https://doi.org/10.1111/cdep.12496.

Harding, K., Galano, J., Martin, J., Huntington, L., & Schellenbach, C. J. (2007). Healthy families America® effectiveness: A comprehensive review of outcomes. *Journal of Prevention & Intervention in the Community, 34*(1–2), 149–179. https://doi.org/10.1300/J005v34n01_08.

Harris, N. B. (2018). *The Deepest Well: Healing the Long-Term Effects of Childhood Adversity*. Houghton Mifflin Harcourt.

Harrison, L. J., & Murray, E. (2015). Stress, coping and wellbeing in kindergarten: Children's perspectives on personal, interpersonal and institutional challenges of school. *International Journal of Early Childhood*, *47*(1), 79–103. https://doi.org/10.1007/s13158-014-0127-4.

Harrison, P. A., & Narayan, G. (2003). Differences in behavior, psychological factors, and environmental factors associated with participation in school sports and other activities in adolescence. *Journal of School Health*, *73*(3), 113–120. https://doi.org/10.1111/j.1746-1561.2003.tb03585.x.

Harrist, A. W., Pettit, G. S., Dodge, K. A., & Bates, J. E. (1994). Dyadic synchrony in mother-child interaction: Relation with children's subsequent kindergarten adjustment. *Family Relations*, *43*(4), 417. https://doi.org/10.2307/585373.

Hartup, W. W. (1996). The company they keep: Friendships and their developmental significance. *Child Development*, *67*(1), 1–13. https://doi.org/10.2307/1131681.

Hartup, W. W., & Abecassis, M. (2002). Friends and enemies. In P. K. Smith & C. H. Hart (Eds.), *Blackwell Handbook of Childhood Social Development* (pp. 286–306). Blackwell.

Hastings, P. D., Ruttle, P. L., Serbin, L. A., et al. (2011). Adrenocortical responses to strangers in preschoolers: Relations with parenting, temperament, and psychopathology. *Developmental Psychobiology*, *53*(7), 694–710. https://doi.org/10.1002/dev.20545.

Havighurst, S. S., Wilson, K. R., Harley, A. E., et al. (2013). "Tuning into Kids": Reducing young children's behavior problems using an emotion coaching parenting program. *Child Psychiatry & Human Development*, *44*(2), 247–264. https://doi.org/10.1007/s10578-012-0322-1.

Haynes, J. D., Marsh, L. T. S., & Anderson, K. M. (2023). Planting the seeds of culturally responsive, equity-centered, and trauma-informed attitudes among urban educators. *Urban Education*, *60*(3). https://doi.org/10.1177/00420859231175663.

Hektner, J. M., August, G. J., Bloomquist, M. L., Lee, S., & Klimes-Dougan, B. (2014). A 10-year randomized controlled trial of the Early Risers conduct problems preventive intervention: Effects on externalizing and internalizing in late high school. *Journal of Consulting and Clinical Psychology*, *82*(2), 355–360. https://doi.org/10.1037/a0035678.

Hentges, R. F., Davies, P. T., & Cicchetti, D. (2015). Temperament and interparental conflict: The role of negative emotionality in predicting child behavioral problems. *Child Development*, *86*(5), 1333–1350. https://doi.org/10.1111/cdev.12389.

Herman, K. C., Hickmon-Rosa, J., & Reinke, W. M. (2018). Empirically derived profiles of teacher stress, burnout, self-efficacy, and coping and associated student outcomes. *Journal of Positive Behavior Interventions*, *20*(2), 90–100. https://doi.org/10.1177/1098300717732066.

Herzberg, M. P., & Gunnar, M. R. (2020). Early life stress and brain function: Activity and connectivity associated with processing emotion and reward. *NeuroImage*, *209*, 116493. https://doi.org/10.1016/j.neuroimage.2019.116493.

Hibel, L. C., Granger, D. A., Blair, C., Finegood, E. D., & Family Life Project Key Investigators. (2015). Maternal-child adrenocortical attunement in early childhood: Continuity and change. *Developmental Psychobiology*, *57*(1), 83–95. https://doi.org/10.1002/dev.21266.

Hinduja, S., & Patchin, J. W. (2023). *Cyberbullying: Identification, Prevention, and Response* (2023 ed.). Cyberbullying Research Center. https://cyberbullying.org.

Hjort, J., Sølvsten, M., & Wüst, M. (2017). Universal investment in infants and long-run health: Evidence from denmark's 1937 home visiting program. *American Economic Journal: Applied Economics*, *9*(4), 78–104. https://doi.org/10.1257/app.20150087.

Hodgdon, H. B., Blaustein, M., Kinniburgh, K., Peterson, M. L., & Spinazzola, J. (2016). Application of the ARC model with adopted children: Supporting resiliency and family well being. *Journal of Child & Adolescent Trauma*, *9*(1), 43–53. https://doi.org/10.1007/s40653-015-0050-3.

Hohl, B. C., Kondo, M. C., Kajeepeta, S., et al. (2019). Creating safe and healthy neighborhoods with place-based violence interventions. *Health Affairs (Project Hope)*, *38*(10), 1687–1694. https://doi.org/10.1377/hlthaff.2019.00707.

Hostinar, C. E., Johnson, A. E., & Gunnar, M. R. (2015a). Early social deprivation and the social buffering of cortisol stress responses in late childhood: An experimental study. *Developmental Psychology*, *51*(11), 1597–1608. https://doi.org/10.1037/dev0000029.

Hostinar, C. E., Johnson, A. E., & Gunnar, M. R. (2015b). Parent support is less effective in buffering cortisol stress reactivity for adolescents compared to children. *Developmental Science*, *18*(2), 281–297. https://doi.org/10.1111/desc.12195.

Hostinar, C. E., & Miller, G. E. (2019). Protective factors for youth confronting economic hardship: Current challenges and future avenues in resilience research. *The American Psychologist, 74*(6), 641–652. https://doi.org/10.1037/amp0000520.

Hostinar, C. E., Stellern, S. A., Schaefer, C., Carlson, S. M., & Gunnar, M. R. (2012). Associations between early life adversity and executive function in children adopted internationally from orphanages. *Proceedings of the National Academy of Sciences of the United States of America, 109*(Suppl 2), 17208–17212. https://doi.org/10.1073/pnas.1121246109.

Hostinar, C. E., Sullivan, R. M., & Gunnar, M. R. (2014). Psychobiological mechanisms underlying the social buffering of the hypothalamic–pituitary–adrenocortical axis: A review of animal models and human studies across development. *Psychological Bulletin, 140*(1), 256–282. https://doi.org/10.1037/a0032671.

Hostinar, C. E., Swartz, J. R., Alen, N. V., Guyer, A. E., & Hastings, P. D. (2023). The role of stress phenotypes in understanding childhood adversity as a transdiagnostic risk factor for psychopathology. *Journal of Psychopathology and Clinical Science, 132*(3), 277–286. https://doi.org/10.1037/abn0000619.

Hoyniak, C. P., Quiñones-Camacho, L. E., Camacho, M. C., et al. (2021). Adversity is linked with decreased parent-child behavioral and neural synchrony. *Developmental Cognitive Neuroscience, 48*, 100937. https://doi.org/10.1016/j.dcn.2021.100937.

Huguley, J. P., Wang, M.-T., Vasquez, A. C., & Guo, J. (2019). Parental ethnic–racial socialization practices and the construction of children of color's ethnic–racial identity: A research synthesis and meta-analysis. *Psychological Bulletin, 145*(5), 437–458. https://doi.org/10.1037/bul0000187.

Humphrey, N., Kalambouka, A., Wigelsworth, M., et al. (2011). Measures of social and emotional skills for children and young people: A systematic review. *Educational and Psychological Measurement, 71*(4), 617–637. https://doi.org/10.1177/0013164410382896.

Humphreys, K. L., & Zeanah, C. H. (2015). Deviations from the expectable environment in early childhood and emerging psychopathology. *Neuropsychopharmacology, 40*(1), 154–170. https://doi.org/10.1038/npp.2014.165.

Hutchings, J., Bywater, T., Daley, D., et al. (2007). Parenting intervention in sure start services for children at risk of developing conduct disorder: Pragmatic randomised controlled trial. *BMJ, 334*(7595), 678. https://doi.org/10.1136/bmj.39126.620799.55.

Intrator, J., Tannen, J., & Massey, D. S. (2016). Segregation by race and income in the United States 1970–2010. *Social Science Research, 60*, 45–60. https://doi.org/10.1016/j.ssresearch.2016.08.003.

Isaac, A. J., Rodriguez, A. M., D'Anna-Hernandez, K., et al. (2023). Preschool-aged children's hair cortisol and parents' behavior, psychopathology, and stress. *Psychoneuroendocrinology, 151*, 106052. https://doi.org/10.1016/j.psyneuen.2023.106052.

Isumi, A., Doi, S., Ochi, M., Kato, T., & Fujiwara, T. (2023). School- and community-level protective factors for resilience among chronically maltreated children in Japan. *Social Psychiatry and Psychiatric Epidemiology, 58*(3), 477–488. https://doi.org/10.1007/s00127-022-02322-x.

Jaffee, S. R., Caspi, A., Moffitt, T. E., Polo-Tomás, M., & Taylor, A. (2007). Individual, family, and neighborhood factors distinguish resilient from non-resilient maltreated children: A cumulative stressors model. *Child Abuse & Neglect, 31*(3), 231–253. https://doi.org/10.1016/j.chiabu.2006.03.011.

Jaffee, S. R., McFarquhar, T., Stevens, S., et al. (2015). Interactive effects of early and recent exposure to stressful contexts on cortisol reactivity in middle childhood. *Journal of Child Psychology and Psychiatry, 56*(2), 138–146. https://doi.org/10.1111/jcpp.12287.

Jennings, P. A., & Greenberg, M. T. (2009). The prosocial classroom: Teacher social and emotional competence in relation to student and classroom outcomes. *Review of Educational Research, 79*(1), 491–525. https://doi.org/10.3102/0034654308325693.

Jeon, L., Buettner, C. K., Grant, A. A., & Lang, S. N. (2019). Early childhood teachers' stress and children's social, emotional, and behavioral functioning. *Journal of Applied Developmental Psychology, 61*, 21–32. https://doi.org/10.1016/j.appdev.2018.02.002.

Jewett, J., & Peterson, K. (2002). *Stress and Young Children. ERIC Digest*. ERIC Clearinghouse on Elementary and Early Childhood Education, Children's Research Center, University of Illinois, 51 Gerty Dr. https://eric.ed.gov/?id=ED471911.

Jiang, H., Justice, L., Purtell, K. M., Lin, T.-J., & Logan, J. (2021). Prevalence and prediction of kindergarten-transition difficulties. *Early Childhood Research Quarterly, 55*, 15–23. https://doi.org/10.1016/j.ecresq.2020.10.006.

Jimenez, M. E., Wade, R., Jr, Lin, Y., Morrow, L. M., & Reichman, N. E. (2016). Adverse experiences in early childhood and kindergarten outcomes. *Pediatrics, 137*(2), e20151839. https://doi.org/10.1542/peds.2015-1839.

Johnson, A. E., Bruce, J., Tarullo, A. R., & Gunnar, M. R. (2011). Growth delay as an index of allostatic load in young children: Predictions to disinhibited social approach and diurnal cortisol activity. *Development and Psychopathology, 23*(3), 859–871. https://doi.org/10.1017/S0954579411000356.

Johnson, J. H. (1982). Life events as stressors in childhood and adolescence. In B. B. Lahey & A. E. Kazdin (Eds.), *Advances in Clinical Child Psychology* (pp. 219–253). Springer US. https://doi.org/10.1007/978-1-4613-9811-0_6.

Johnston-Brooks, C. H., Lewis, M. A., Evans, G. W., & Whalen, C. K. (1998). Chronic stress and illness in children: The role of allostatic load. *Psychosomatic Medicine*, *60*(5), 597–603. https://doi.org/10.1097/00006842-199809000-00015.

Jones, S. M., & Doolittle, E. J. (2017). Social and emotional learning: Introducing the issue. *The Future of Children*, *27*(1), 3–11.

Jost, G. M., Hang, S., Shaikh, U., & Hostinar, C. E. (2023). Understanding adolescent stress during the COVID-19 pandemic. *Current Opinion in Psychology*, *52*, 101646. https://doi.org/10.1016/j.copsyc.2023.101646.

Jutte, D. P., Miller, J. L., & Erickson, D. J. (2015). Neighborhood adversity, child health, and the role for community development. *Pediatrics*, *135* (Supplement_2), S48–S57. https://doi.org/10.1542/peds.2014-3549F.

Juvonen, J., Nishina, A., & Graham, S. (2006). Ethnic diversity and perceptions of safety in urban middle schools. *Psychological Science*, *17*(5), 393–400. https://doi.org/10.1111/j.1467-9280.2006.01718.x.

Kalvin, C. B., Bierman, K. L., & Gatzke-Kopp, L. M. (2016). Emotional reactivity, behavior problems, and social adjustment at school entry in a high-risk sample. *Journal of Abnormal Child Psychology*, *44*(8), 1527–1541. https://doi.org/10.1007/s10802-016-0139-7.

Kearney, C. A. (2003). Bridging the gap among professionals who address youths with school absenteeism: Overview and suggestions for consensus. *Professional Psychology: Research and Practice*, *34*(1), 57–65. https://doi.org/10.1037/0735-7028.34.1.57.

Kearney, C. A. (2008). School absenteeism and school refusal behavior in youth: A contemporary review. *Clinical Psychology Review*, *28*(3), 451–471. https://doi.org/10.1016/j.cpr.2007.07.012.

Kessler, R. C., McLaughlin, K. A., Green, J. G., et al. (2010). Childhood adversities and adult psychopathology in the WHO World Mental Health Surveys. *British Journal of Psychiatry*, *197*(5), 378–385. https://doi.org/10.1192/bjp.bp.110.080499.

Khang, Y.-H., June, K. J., Park, S. E., et al. (2022). Is a universal nurse home visiting program possible? A cross-sectional survey of nurse home visitation service needs among pregnant women and mothers with young children. *PLoS ONE*, *17*(8), e0272227. https://doi.org/10.1371/journal.pone.0272227.

Kimbro, R. T., Brooks-Gunn, J., & McLanahan, S. (2011). Young children in urban areas: Links among neighborhood characteristics, weight status, outdoor play, and television watching. *Social Science & Medicine*, *72*(5), 668–676. https://doi.org/10.1016/j.socscimed.2010.12.015.

King, N. J., & Bernstein, G. A. (2001). School refusal in children and adolescents: A review of the past 10 years. *Journal of the American Academy of*

Child & Adolescent Psychiatry, 40(2), 197–205. https://doi.org/10.1097/00004583-200102000-00014.

Kiyimba, N., & O'Reilly, M. (2020). The clinical use of subjective units of distress scales (SUDs) in child mental health assessments: A thematic evaluation. *Journal of Mental Health, 29*(4), 418–423. https://doi.org/10.1080/09638237.2017.1340616.

Kliewer, W., Sosnowski, D. W., Noh, H., McGuire, K., & Wright, A. W. (2019). Peer victimization and cortisol production in children and adolescents: A systematic review. *Journal of Applied Biobehavioral Research, 24*(4), e12172. https://doi.org/10.1111/jabr.12172.

Koss, K. J., Lawler, J. M., & Gunnar, M. R. (2020). Early adversity and children's regulatory deficits: Does post-adoption parenting facilitate recovery in post-institutionalized children? *Development and Psychopathology, 32*(3), 879–896. https://doi.org/10.1017/S0954579419001226.

Koss, K. J., Mliner, S. B., Donzella, B., & Gunnar, M. R. (2016). Early adversity, hypocortisolism, and behavior problems at school entry: A study of internationally adopted children. *Psychoneuroendocrinology, 66*, 31–38. https://doi.org/10.1016/j.psyneuen.2015.12.018.

Kuhlman, K. R., Repetti, R. L., Reynolds, B. M., & Robles, T. F. (2016). Change in parent-child conflict and the HPA-axis: Where should we be looking and for how long? *Psychoneuroendocrinology, 68*, 74–81. https://doi.org/10.1016/j.psyneuen.2016.02.029.

Ladd, G. W., & Burgess, K. B. (2001). Do relational risks and protective factors moderate the linkages between childhood aggression and early psychological and school adjustment? *Child Development, 72*(5), 1579–1601. https://doi.org/10.1111/1467-8624.00366.

Ladd, G. W., Kochenderfer-Ladd, B., Eggum, N. D., Kochel, K. P., & McConnell, E. M. (2011).Characterizing and comparing the friendships of anxious-solitary and unsociable preadolescents. *Child Development, 82*(5), 1434–1453. https://doi.org/10.1111/j.1467-8624.2011.01632.x.

Lagattuta, K. H. (2005). When you shouldn't do what you want to do: Young children's understanding of desires, rules, and emotions. *Child Development, 76*(3), 713–733. https://doi.org/10.1111/j.1467-8624.2005.00873.x.

Langley, A. K., Gonzalez, A., Sugar, C. A., Solis, D., & Jaycox, L. (2015). Bounce back: Effectiveness of an elementary school-based intervention for multicultural children exposed to traumatic events. *Journal of Consulting and Clinical Psychology, 83*(5), 853–865. https://doi.org/10.1037/ccp0000051.

Lazarus, R. S., & Folkman, S. (1984). *Stress, Appraisal, and Coping*. Springer.

Lengua, L. J., Gartstein, M. A., Zhou, Q., Colder, C. R., & Jacques, D. T. (2024). *Temperament and Child Development in Context*. Cambridge University Press.

Levy, D. J., Heissel, J. A., Richeson, J. A., & Adam, E. K. (2016). Psychological and biological responses to race-based social stress as pathways to disparities in educational outcomes. *American Psychologist*, *71*(6), 455–473. https://doi.org/10.1037/a0040322.

Lewallen, A. C., & Neece, C. L. (2015). Improved social skills in children with developmental delays after parent participation in MBSR: The role of parent–child relational factors. *Journal of Child and Family Studies*, *24*(10), 3117–3129. https://doi.org/10.1007/s10826-015-0116-8.

Li, Y., Jia, W., Yan, N., et al. (2023). Associations between chronic stress and hair cortisol in children: A systematic review and meta-analysis. *Journal of Affective Disorders*, *329*, 438–447. https://doi.org/10.1016/j.jad.2023.02.123.

Li, Y., Li, H., Decety, J., & Lee, K. (2013). Experiencing a natural disaster alters children's altruistic giving. *Psychological Science*, *24*(9), 1686–1695. https://doi.org/10.1177/0956797613479975.

Lieberman, A. F., Horn, P. V., & Ippen, C. G. (2005). Toward evidence-based treatment: Child-parent psychotherapy with preschoolers exposed to marital violence. *Journal of the American Academy of Child & Adolescent Psychiatry*, *44*(12), 1241–1248. https://doi.org/10.1097/01.chi.0000181047.59702.58.

Liberman, Z., & Shaw, A. (2019). Children use similarity, propinquity, and loyalty to predict which people are friends. *Journal of Experimental Child Psychology*, *184*, 1–17. https://doi.org/10.1016/j.jecp.2019.03.002.

Lieberman, A. F., & Van Horn, P. (2004). *Don't Hit my Mommy: A Manual for Child Parent Psychotherapy with Young Witnesses of Family Violence*. Zero to Three Press.

Lisonbee, J. A., Mize, J., Payne, A. L., & Granger, D. A. (2008). Children's cortisol and the quality of teacher–child relationships in child care. *Child Development*, *79*(6), 1818–1832. https://doi.org/10.1111/j.1467-8624.2008.01228.x.

Liu, V., & Cimpian, A. (2025). In the United States, children are more likely than adults to condone discrimination. *Cognitive Psychology*, *156*, 101703. https://doi.org/10.1016/j.cogpsych.2024.101703.

Liu, C. H., & Doan, S. N. (2020). Psychosocial stress contagion in children and families during the COVID-19 pandemic. *Clinical Pediatrics*, *59*(9–10), 853–855. https://doi.org/10.1177/0009922820927044.

Liu, S., Fisher, P. A., Schlueter, L. J., et al. (2021). A brief video-coaching intervention buffers young children's vulnerability to the impact of caregivers' depressive symptoms: Examination of differential susceptibility.

Development and Psychopathology, *33*(5), 1685–1700. https://doi.org/10.1017/S0954579421000687.

Lobo, F. M., & Lunkenheimer, E. (2020). Understanding the parent-child coregulation patterns shaping child self-regulation. *Developmental Psychology*, *56*(6), 1121–1134. https://doi.org/10.1037/dev0000926.

Lowell, D. I., Carter, A. S., Godoy, L., Paulicin, B., & Briggs-Gowan, M. J. (2011). A randomized controlled trial of child FIRST: A comprehensive home-based intervention translating research into early childhood practice. *Child Development*, *82*(1), 193–208. https://doi.org/10.1111/j.1467-8624.2010.01550.x.

Lucas-Thompson, R. G., & Goldberg, W. A. (2011). Family relationships and children's stress responses. In J. B. Benson (Ed.), *Advances in Child Development and Behavior* (Vol. 40, pp. 243–299). JAI. https://doi.org/10.1016/B978-0-12-386491-8.00007-4.

Lund, J. I., Toombs, E., Radford, A., Boles, K., & Mushquash, C. (2020). Adverse childhood experiences and executive function difficulties in children: A systematic review. *Child Abuse & Neglect*, *106*, 104485. https://doi.org/10.1016/j.chiabu.2020.104485.

Lunkenheimer, E., Ram, N., Skowron, E. A., & Yin, P. (2017). Harsh parenting, child behavior problems, and the dynamic coupling of parents' and children's positive behaviors. *Journal of Family Psychology*, *31*(6), 689–698. https://doi.org/10.1037/fam0000310.

Luthar, S. S. (2003). The culture of affluence: Psychological costs of material wealth. *Child Development*, *74*(6), 1581–1593. https://doi.org/10.1046/j.1467-8624.2003.00625.x.

Luthar, S. S., & Becker, B. E. (2002). Privileged but Pressured? A study of affluent youth. *Child Development*, *73*(5), 1593–1610. https://doi.org/10.1111/1467-8624.00492.

Luthar, S. S., Doernberger, C. H., & Zigler, E. (1993). Resilience is not a unidimensional construct: Insights from a prospective study of inner-city adolescents. *Development and Psychopathology*, *5*(4), 703–717. https://doi.org/10.1017/S0954579400006246.

Luthar, S. S., & Goldstein, A. (2004). Children's exposure to community violence: Implications for understanding risk and resilience. *Journal of Clinical Child and Adolescent Psychology : The Official Journal for the Society of Clinical Child and Adolescent Psychology, American Psychological Association, Division 53*, *33*(3), 499–505. https://doi.org/10.1207/s15374424jccp3303_7.

Luthar, S. S., & Latendresse, S. J. (2005). Children of the affluent: Challenges to well-being. *Current Directions in Psychological Science*, *14*(1), 49–53. https://doi.org/10.1111/j.0963-7214.2005.00333.x.

Lynch, T., Davis, S. L., Johnson, A. H., et al. (2022). Definitions, theories, and measurement of stress in children. *Journal of Pediatric Nursing, 66,* 202–212. https://doi.org/10.1016/j.pedn.2022.07.008.

Machlin, L., Miller, A. B., Snyder, J., McLaughlin, K. A., & Sheridan, M. A. (2019). Differential associations of deprivation and threat with cognitive control and fear conditioning in early childhood. *Frontiers in Behavioral Neuroscience, 13,* 80. https://doi.org/10.3389/fnbeh.2019.00080.

MacKenzie, M. J., Nicklas, E., Brooks-Gunn, J., & Waldfogel, J. (2015). Spanking and children's externalizing behavior across the first decade of life: Evidence for transactional processes. *Journal of Youth and Adolescence, 44*(3), 658–669. https://doi.org/10.1007/s10964-014-0114-y.

MacKinnon, A. L., Tomfohr-Madsen, L., & Tough, S. (2020). Neighborhood socio-economic factors and associations with infant sleep health. *Behavioral Sleep Medicine, 19*(4), 458–470. https://doi.org/10.1080/15402002.2020.1778478.

Maercker, A. (2021). Development of the new CPTSD diagnosis for ICD-11. *Borderline Personality Disorder and Emotion Dysregulation, 8*(1), 7. https://doi.org/10.1186/s40479-021-00148-8.

Maguire-Jack, K., & Showalter, K. (2016). The protective effect of neighborhood social cohesion in child abuse and neglect. *Child Abuse & Neglect, 52,* 29–37. https://doi.org/10.1016/j.chiabu.2015.12.011.

Maier, S. F., & Watkins, L. R. (2010). Role of the medial prefrontal cortex in coping and resilience. *Brain Research, 1355,* 52–60. https://doi.org/10.1016/j.brainres.2010.08.039.

Marcelo, A. K., & Yates, T. M. (2019). Young children's ethnic–racial identity moderates the impact of early discrimination experiences on child behavior problems. *Cultural Diversity and Ethnic Minority Psychology, 25*(2), 253–265. https://doi.org/10.1037/cdp0000220.

Martin, C. G., Kim, H. K., Bruce, J., & Fisher, P. A. (2014). Child diurnal cortisol rhythms, parenting quality, and externalizing behaviors in preadolescence. *Psychoneuroendocrinology, 40,* 170–180. https://doi.org/10.1016/j.psyneuen.2013.11.015.

Marzano, R. J., & Marzano, J. S. (2003). *Classroom Management That Works: Research-Based Strategies for Every Teacher.* ASCD.

Masarik, A. S., & Conger, R. D. (2017). Stress and child development: A review of the family stress model. *Current Opinion in Psychology, 13,* 85–90. https://doi.org/10.1016/j.copsyc.2016.05.008.

Maschi, T., Perez, R. M., & Tyson, E. (2010). Exploring the relationship between exposure to violence, perceptions of neighborhood safety, and children's adaptive functioning: Clinical and community implications.

Journal of Human Behavior in the Social Environment, 20(6), 744–761. https://doi.org/10.1080/10911351003749144.

Masten, A. S. (2018). Resilience theory and research on children and families: Past, present, and promise. *Journal of Family Theory & Review, 10*(1), 12–31. https://doi.org/10.1111/jftr.12255.

Masten, A. S., & Barnes, A. J. (2018). Resilience in children: Developmental perspectives. *Children, 5*(7), 98. https://doi.org/10.3390/children5070098.

Masten, A. S., Garmezy, N., Tellegen, A., et al. (1988). Competence and stress in school children: The moderating effects of individual and family qualities. *Journal of Child Psychology and Psychiatry, 29*(6), 745–764. https://doi.org/10.1111/j.1469-7610.1988.tb00751.x.

Matheny, A. P., Wachs, T. D., Ludwig, J. L., & Phillips, K. (1995). Bringing order out of chaos: Psychometric characteristics of the confusion, hubbub, and order scale. *Journal of Applied Developmental Psychology, 16*(3), 429–444. https://doi.org/10.1016/0193-3973(95)90028-4.

Mathewson, K. J., Miskovic, V., Cunningham, C. E., et al. (2012). Salivary cortisol, socioemotional functioning, and academic performance in anxious and non-anxious children of elementary and middle school age: Early education & development. *Early Education & Development, 23*(1), 74–95. https://doi.org/10.1080/10409289.2012.626388.

Maxwell, L. E. (2010). Chaos outside the home: The school environment. In G. W. Evans & T. D. Wachs (Eds.), *Chaos and Its Influence on Children's Development: An Ecological Perspective* (pp. 83–95). American Psychological Association. https://doi.org/10.1037/12057-006.

McEwen, B. (2000). Stress, definition and concepts of. In G. Fink (Ed.), *Encyclopedia of Stress* (Vol. 3, pp. 508–509). Academic Press.

McEwen, B. S. (2007). Physiology and neurobiology of stress and adaptation: Central role of the brain. *Physiological Reviews, 87*(3), 873–904. https://doi.org/10.1152/physrev.00041.2006.

McEwen, B. S., & Akil, H. (2020). Revisiting the stress concept: Implications for affective disorders. *Journal of Neuroscience, 40*(1), 12–21. https://doi.org/10.1523/JNEUROSCI.0733-19.2019.

McEwen, B. S., & Wingfield, J. C. (2010). What's in a name? Integrating homeostasis, allostasis and stress. *Hormones and Behavior, 57*(2), 105. https://doi.org/10.1016/j.yhbeh.2009.09.011.

McGinnis, R. S., McGinnis, E. W., Hruschak, J., et al. (2018). Rapid anxiety and depression diagnosis in young children enabled by wearable sensors and machine learning. *2018 40th Annual International Conference of the IEEE Engineering in Medicine and Biology Society (EMBC)*, 3983–3986. https://doi.org/10.1109/EMBC.2018.8513327.

McLaughlin, K. A., Sheridan, M. A., Humphreys, K. L., Belsky, J., & Ellis, B. J. (2021). The value of dimensional models of early experience: Thinking clearly about concepts and categories. *Perspectives on Psychological Science*, *16*(6), 1463–1472. https://doi.org/10.1177/1745691621992346.

McLaughlin, K. A., Sheridan, M. A., Tibu, F., et al. (2015). Causal effects of the early caregiving environment on development of stress response systems in children. *Proceedings of the National Academy of Sciences*, *112*(18), 5637–5642. https://doi.org/10.1073/pnas.1423363112.

McLaughlin, K. A., Weissman, D., & Bitrán, D. (2019). Childhood adversity and neural development: A systematic review. *Annual Review of Developmental Psychology*, *1*, 277–312. https://doi.org/10.1146/annurev-devpsych-121318-084950.

McLeigh, J. D., McDonell, J. R., & Lavenda, O. (2018). Neighborhood poverty and child abuse and neglect: The mediating role of social cohesion. *Children and Youth Services Review*, *93*, 154–160. https://doi.org/10.1016/j.childyouth.2018.07.018.

McLoyd, V. C. (1998). Socioeconomic disadvantage and child development. *American Psychologist*, 53(2), 185–204.

Meiklejohn, J., Phillips, C., Freedman, M. L., et al. (2012). Integrating mindfulness training into K-12 education: Fostering the resilience of teachers and students. *Mindfulness*, *3*(4), 291–307. https://doi.org/10.1007/s12671-012-0094-5.

Mendes, W. B. (2009). Assessing the autonomic nervous system. In E. Harmon-Jones & J. S. Beer (Eds.), *Methods in Social Neuroscience* (pp. 118–147). The Guilford Press.

Menezes, M., Soland, J., & Mazurek, M. O. (2024). Association between neighborhood support and family resilience in households with autistic children. *Journal of Autism and Developmental Disorders*, *54*(5), 1765–1773. https://doi.org/10.1007/s10803-023-05951-6.

Meyer, I. H. (2003). Prejudice, social stress, and mental health in lesbian, gay, and bisexual populations: Conceptual issues and research sevidence. *Psychological Bulletin*, *129*(5), 674–697. https://doi.org/10.1037/0033-2909.129.5.674.

Meyer, J. S., & Novak, M. A. (2012). Minireview: Hair cortisol: A novel biomarker of hypothalamic-pituitary-adrenocortical activity. *Endocrinology*, *153*(9), 4120–4127. https://doi.org/10.1210/en.2012-1226.

Milam, A. J., Furr-Holden, C. D. M., & Leaf, P. J. (2010). Perceived school and neighborhood safety, neighborhood violence and academic achievement in urban school children. *The Urban Review*, *42*(5), 458–467. https://doi.org/10.1007/s11256-010-0165-7.

Miller, G. E., & Chen, E. (2013). The biological residue of childhood poverty. *Child Development Perspectives*, *7*(2), 67–73. https://doi.org/10.1111/cdep.12021.

Miller, G. E., Chen, E., & Parker, K. J. (2011). Psychological stress in childhood and susceptibility to the chronic diseases of aging: Moving toward a model of behavioral and biological mechanisms. *Psychological Bulletin*, *137*(6), 959–997. https://doi.org/10.1037/a0024768.

Miller, G. E., Chen, E., & Zhou, E. S. (2007). If it goes up, must it come down? Chronic stress and the hypothalamic-pituitary-adrenocortical axis in humans. *Psychological Bulletin*, *133*(1), 25–45. https://doi.org/10.1037/0033-2909.133.1.25.

Mistry, R. S., Vandewater, E. A., Huston, A. C., & McLoyd, V. C. (2002). Economic well-being and children's social adjustment: The role of family process in an ethnically diverse low-income sample. *Child Development*, *73*(3), 935–951. https://doi.org/10.1111/1467-8624.00448.

Miu, A. C., Szentágotai-Tătar, A., Balázsi, R., et al. (2022). Emotion regulation as mediator between childhood adversity and psychopathology: A meta-analysis. *Clinical Psychology Review*, *93*, 102141. https://doi.org/10.1016/j.cpr.2022.102141.

Morgan Hughey, S., Kaczynski, A. T., Child, S., et al. (2017). Green and lean: Is neighborhood park and playground availability associated with youth obesity? Variations by gender, socioeconomic status, and race/ethnicity. *Preventive Medicine*, *95*, S101–S108. https://doi.org/10.1016/j.ypmed.2016.11.024.

Morris, A. S., Criss, M. M., Silk, J. S., & Houltberg, B. J. (2017). The impact of parenting on emotion regulation during childhood and adolescence. *Child Development Perspectives*, *11*(4), 233–238. https://doi.org/10.1111/cdep.12238.

Mulligan, D. J., Palopoli, A. C., van den Heuvel, M. I., Thomason, M. E., & Trentacosta, C. J. (2022). Frontal alpha asymmetry in response to stressor moderates the relation between parenting hassles and child externalizing problems. *Frontiers in Neuroscience*, *16*. https://doi.org/10.3389/fnins.2022.917300.

Muniz, C. N., Fox, B., Miley, L. N., et al. (2019). The effects of adverse childhood experiences on internalizing versus externalizing outcomes. *Criminal Justice and Behavior*, *46*(4), 568–589. https://doi.org/10.1177/0093854819826213.

Nachmias, M., Gunnar, M., Mangelsdorf, S., Parritz, R. H., & Buss, K. (1996). Behavioral inhibition and stress reactivity: The moderating role of attachment security. *Child Development*, *67*(2), 508–522.

National Child Traumatic Stress Network (2024a). What is a traumatic event? Retrieved August 15, 2024, www.nctsn.org/what-is-child-trauma/about-child-trauma.

National Child Traumatic Stress Network (2024b). Interventions. Retrieved May 31, 2025, www.nctsn.org/treatments-and-practices/trauma-treatments/interventions.

Negriff, S., Gordis, E. B., Susman, E. J., et al. (2020). The young adolescent project: A longitudinal study of the effects of maltreatment on adolescent development. *Development and Psychopathology*, *32*, 1440–1459. https://doi.org/10.1017/S0954579419001391.

Nievar, M. A., Moske, A. K., Johnson, D. J., & Chen, Q. (2014). Parenting practices in preschool leading to later cognitive competence: A family stress model. *Early Education and Development*, *25*(3), 318–337. https://doi.org/10.1080/10409289.2013.788426.

Nijhof, S. L., Vinkers, C. H., van Geelen, S. M., et al. (2018). Healthy play, better coping: The importance of play for the development of children in health and disease. *Neuroscience & Biobehavioral Reviews*, *95*, 421–429. https://doi.org/10.1016/j.neubiorev.2018.09.024.

Novick, A. M., Levandowski, M. L., Laumann, L. E., et al. (2018). The effects of early life stress on reward processing. *Journal of Psychiatric Research*, *101*, 80–103. https://doi.org/10.1016/j.jpsychires.2018.02.002.

O'Callaghan, P., McMullen, J., Shannon, C., Rafferty, H., & Black, A. (2013). A randomized controlled trial of trauma-focused cognitive behavioral therapy for sexually exploited, war-affected congolese girls. *Journal of the American Academy of Child & Adolescent Psychiatry*, *52*(4), 359–369. https://doi.org/10.1016/j.jaac.2013.01.013.

Oberle, E., & Schonert-Reichl, K. A. (2016). Stress contagion in the classroom? The link between classroom teacher burnout and morning cortisol in elementary school students. *Social Science & Medicine*, *159*, 30–37. https://doi.org/10.1016/j.socscimed.2016.04.031.

Obradović, J., & Armstrong-Carter, E. (2020). Addressing educational inequalities and promoting learning through studies of stress physiology in elementary school students. *Development and Psychopathology*, *32*(5), 1899–1913. https://doi.org/10.1017/S0954579420001443.

Olds, D. L. (2006). The nurse–family partnership: An evidence-based preventive intervention. *Infant Mental Health Journal*, *27*(1), 5–25. https://doi.org/10.1002/imhj.20077.

Olds, D. L., Kitzman, H., Anson, E., et al. (2019). Prenatal and infancy nurse home visiting effects on mothers: 18-year follow-up of a randomized trial. *Pediatrics*, *144*(6), e20183889. https://doi.org/10.1542/peds.2018-3889.

Olweus, D., & Limber, S. P. (2010). Bullying in school: Evaluation and dissemination of the olweus bullying prevention program. *American Journal of Orthopsychiatry, 80*(1), 124–134. https://doi.org/10.1111/j.1939-0025.2010.01015.x.

Overstreet, S., & Mathews, T. (2011). Challenges associated with exposure to chronic trauma: Using a public health framework to foster resilient outcomes among youth. *Psychology in the Schools, 48*(7), 738–754. https://doi.org/10.1002/pits.20584.

Oxford, M. L., Hash, J. B., Lohr, M. J., et al. (2021). Randomized trial of promoting first relationships for new mothers who received community mental health services in pregnancy. *Developmental Psychology, 57*(8), 1228–1241. https://doi.org/10.1037/dev0001219.

Pandey, A., Hale, D., Das, S., Goddings, A.-L., Blakemore, S.-J., & Viner, R. M. (2018). Effectiveness of universal self-regulation–based interventions in children and adolescents. *JAMA Pediatrics, 172*(6), 566–575. https://doi.org/10.1001/jamapediatrics.2018.0232.

Pang, D., Frydenberg, E., Liang, R., Deans, J., & Su, L. (2018). Improving coping skills and promoting social and emotional competence in pre-schoolers: A pilotSstudy on COPE-R program. *Journal of Early Childhood Education Research, 7*(2), Article 2.

Parent, S., Lupien, S., Herba, C. M., Dupéré, V., Gunnar, M. R., & Séguin, J. R. (2019). Children's cortisol response to the transition from preschool to formal schooling: A review. *Psychoneuroendocrinology, 99*, 196–205. https://doi.org/10.1016/j.psyneuen.2018.09.013.

Parenteau, A. M., Alen, N. V., Deer, L. K., et al. (2020). Parenting matters: Parents can reduce or amplify children's anxiety and cortisol responses to acute stress. *Development and Psychopathology, 32*(5), 1799–1809. https://doi.org/10.1017/S0954579420001285.

Parenteau, A. M., Boyer, C. J., Campos, L. J., et al. (2023). A review of mental health disparities during COVID-19: Evidence, mechanisms, and policy recommendations for promoting societal resilience. *Development and Psychopathology, 35*(4), 1821–1842. https://doi.org/10.1017/S0954579422000499.

Patterson, G. R. (1982). *Coercive Family Process*. Castalia. https://cir.nii.ac.jp/crid/1130282268968068608.

Patterson, G. R. (2002). The early development of coercive family process. In J. B. Reid, G. R. Patterson, & J. Snyder (Eds.), *Antisocial Behavior in Children and Adolescents: A Developmental Analysis and Model for Intervention* (pp. 25–44). American Psychological Association. https://doi.org/10.1037/10468-002.

Pauker, K., Williams, A., & Steele, J. R. (2016). Children's racial categorization in context. *Child Development Perspectives*, *10*(1), 33–38. https://doi.org/10.1111/cdep.12155.

Payton, J., Weissberg, R. P., Durlak, J. A., et al.(2008). The positive impact of social and emotional learning for kindergarten to eighth-grade students: Findings from three scientific reviews. Technical report. In *Collaborative for Academic, Social, and Emotional Learning (NJ1)*. Collaborative for Academic, Social, and Emotional Learning. https://eric.ed.gov/?id=ED505370

Pedersen, S., Vitaro, F., Barker, E. D., & Borge, A. I. H. (2007). The timing of middle-childhood peer rejection and friendship: Linking early behavior to early-adolescent adjustment. *Child Development*, *78*(4), 1037–1051. https://doi.org/10.1111/j.1467-8624.2007.01051.x.

Perdue, N. H., Manzeske, D. P., & Estell, D. B. (2009). Early predictors of school engagement: Exploring the role of peer relationships. *Psychology in the Schools*, *46*(10), 1084–1097. https://doi.org/10.1002/pits.20446.

Pérez-del-Pulgar, C., Anguelovski, I., Cole, H. V. S., et al. (2021). The relationship between residential proximity to outdoor play spaces and children's mental and behavioral health: The importance of neighborhood socioeconomic characteristics. *Environmental Research*, *200*, 111326. https://doi.org/10.1016/j.envres.2021.111326.

Peters, E., Riksen-Walraven, J. M., Cillessen, A. H. N., & de Weerth, C. (2011). Peer rejection and HPA activity in middle childhood: Friendship makes a difference. *Child Development*, *82*(6), 1906–1920. https://doi.org/10.1111/j.1467-8624.2011.01647.x.

Peverill, M., Rosen, M. L., Lurie, L. A., et al. (2023). Childhood trauma and brain structure in children and adolescents. *Developmental Cognitive Neuroscience*, *59*, 101180. https://doi.org/10.1016/j.dcn.2022.101180.

Pianta, R. C. (1999). *Enhancing Relationships between Children and Teachers*. American Psychological Association. http://archive.org/details/enhancingrelatio0000pian.

Priest, N., Doery, K., Lim, C. K., et al. (2024). Racism and health and wellbeing among children and youth–An updated systematic review and meta-analysis. *Social Science & Medicine*, *361*, 117324. https://doi.org/10.1016/j.socscimed.2024.117324.

Priest, N., Paradies, Y., Trenerry, B., et al. (2013). A systematic review of studies examining the relationship between reported racism and health and wellbeing for children and young people. *Social Science & Medicine*, *95*, 115–127.

Prinz, R. J., Sanders, M. R., Shapiro, C. J., Whitaker, D. J., & Lutzker, J. R. (2009). Population-based prevention of child maltreatment: The U.S. triple

P system population trial. *Prevention Science*, *10*(1), 1–12. https://doi.org/10.1007/s11121-009-0123-3.

Quas, J. A., Rush, E. B., Yim, I. S., & Nikolayev, M. (2013). Effects of stress on memory in children and adolescents: Testing causal connections. *Memory*, *22*(6), 616–632. https://doi.org/10.1080/09658211.2013.809766.

Quesada, A. A., Wiemers, U. S., Schoofs, D., & Wolf, O. T. (2012). Psychosocial stress exposure impairs memory retrieval in children. *Psychoneuroendocrinology*, *37*(1), 125–136. https://doi.org/10.1016/j.psyneuen.2011.05.013.

Quigley, K. S., Gianaros, P. J., Norman, G. J., et al. (2024). Publication guidelines for human heart rate and heart rate variability studies in psychophysiology-Part 1: Physiological underpinnings and foundations of measurement. *Psychophysiology*, *61*(9), e14604. https://doi.org/10.1111/psyp.14604.

Quigley, K. M., & Moore, G. A. (2018). Development of cardiac autonomic balance in infancy and early childhood: A possible pathway to mental and physical health outcomes. *Developmental Review*, *49*, 41–61. https://doi.org/10.1016/j.dr.2018.06.004.

Rab, S. L., & Admon, R. (2021). Parsing inter- and intra-individual variability in key nervous system mechanisms of stress responsivity and across functional domains. *Neuroscience and Biobehavioral Reviews*, *120*, 550–564. https://doi.org/10.1016/j.neubiorev.2020.09.007.

Raver, C. C. (2002). Emotions matter: Making the case for the role of young children's emotional development for early school readiness. *Social Policy Report*, *16*(3), 1–20. https://doi.org/10.1002/j.2379-3988.2002.tb00041.x.

Repetti, R. L., Taylor, S. E., & Seeman, T. E. (2002). Risky families: Family social environments and the mental and physical health of offspring. *Psychological Bulletin*, *128*(2), 330–366. https://doi.org/10.1037/0033-2909.128.2.330.

Ribeiro, A. I., Tavares, C., Guttentag, A., & Barros, H. (2019). Association between neighbourhood green space and biological markers in school-aged children. Findings from the Generation XXI birth cohort. *Environment International*, *132*, 105070. https://doi.org/10.1016/j.envint.2019.105070.

Riggs, J. L., Rosenblum, K. L., Muzik, M., et al. (2022). Infant mental health home visiting mitigates impact of maternal adverse childhood experiences on toddler language competence: A randomized controlled trial. *Journal of Developmental & Behavioral Pediatrics*, *43*(4), e227. https://doi.org/10.1097/DBP.0000000000001020.

Rimm-Kaufman, S. E., & Pianta, R. C. (2000). An ecological perspective on the transition to kindergarten: A theoretical framework to guide empirical research. *Journal of Applied Developmental Psychology*, *21*(5), 491–511. https://doi.org/10.1016/S0193-3973(00)00051-4.

Rosenblum, K., Lawler, J., Alfafara, E., et al. (2018). Improving maternal representations in high-risk mothers: A randomized, controlled trial of the mom power parenting intervention. *Child Psychiatry & Human Development*, *49*(3), 372–384. https://doi.org/10.1007/s10578-017-0757-5.

Roubinov, D. S., Hagan, M. J., Boyce, W. T., Adler, N. E., & Bush, N. R. (2018). Family socioeconomic status, cortisol, and physical health in early childhood: The role of advantageous neighborhood characteristics. *Psychosomatic Medicine*, *80*(5), 492. https://doi.org/10.1097/PSY.0000000000000585.

Rubin, K. H., Althoff, R. R., Walkup, J. T., & Hudziak, J. J. (2013). Cross-informant agreement on child and adolescent withdrawn behavior: A latent class approach. *Child Psychiatry & Human Development*, *44*(3), 361–369. https://doi.org/10.1007/s10578-012-0330-1.

Rubin, K. H., & Chronis-Tuscano, A. (2021). Perspectives on social withdrawal in childhood: Past, present, and prospects. *Child Development Perspectives*, *15*(3), 160–167. https://doi.org/10.1111/cdep.12417.

Rubin, K. H., & Coplan, R. J. (2004). Paying attention to and not neglecting social withdrawal and social isolation. Merrill-Palmer Q. 50(506–34).

Rubin, K. H., Coplan, R. J., & Bowker, J. C. (2009). Social withdrawal in childhood. *Annual Review of Psychology*, *60*(1), 141–171. https://doi.org/10.1146/annurev.psych.60.110707.163642.

Rubin, K. H., Coplan, R., Chen, X., Bowker, J., & McDonald, K. L. (2011). Peer relationships in childhood. In M. H. Bornstein & M. E. Lamb (Eds.), *Developmental Science: An Advanced Textbook* (6th ed., pp. 519–570). Psychology Press.

Rudolph, K. D., & Hammen, C. (1999). Age and gender as determinants of stress exposure, generation, and reactions in youngsters: A transactional perspective. *Child Development*, *70*(3), 660–677. https://doi.org/10.1111/1467-8624.00048.

Russ, S. J., Herbert, J., Cooper, P., et al. (2012). Cortisol levels in response to starting school in children at increased risk for social phobia. *Psychoneuroendocrinology*, *37*(4), 462–474. https://doi.org/10.1016/j.psyneuen.2011.07.014.

Sahle, B. W., Reavley, N. J., Li, W., et al. (2022). The association between adverse childhood experiences and common mental disorders and suicidality: An umbrella review of systematic reviews and meta-analyses. *European Child & Adolescent Psychiatry*, *31*(10), 1489–1499. https://doi.org/10.1007/s00787-021-01745-2.

Sanders, M. R., Kirby, J. N., Tellegen, C. L., & Day, J. J. (2014). The triple P-positive parenting program: A systematic review and meta-analysis of a multi-level system of parenting support. *Clinical Psychology Review, 34*(4), 337–357. https://doi.org/10.1016/j.cpr.2014.04.003.

Scheeringa, M. S., Weems, C. F., Cohen, J. A., Amaya-Jackson, L., & Guthrie, D. (2011). Trauma-focused cognitive-behavioral therapy for post-traumatic stress disorder in three-through six year-old children: A randomized clinical trial. *Journal of Child Psychology and Psychiatry, 52*(8), 853–860. https://doi.org/10.1111/j.1469-7610.2010.02354.x.

Schonert-Reichl, K. A., Oberle, E., Lawlor, M. S., et al. (2015). Enhancing cognitive and social–emotional development through a simple-to-administer mindfulness-based school program for elementary school children: A randomized controlled trial. *Developmental Psychology, 51*(1), 52–66. https://doi.org/10.1037/a0038454.

Schwabe, L., Joëls, M., Roozendaal, B., Wolf, O. T., & Oitzl, M. S. (2012). Stress effects on memory: an update and integration. *Neuroscience and biobehavioral reviews, 36*(7), 1740–1749. https://doi.org/10.1016/j.neubiorev.2011.07.002.

Schwartz, A. E., Laurito, A., Lacoe, J., Sharkey, P., & Ellen, I. G. (2022). The academic effects of chronic exposure to neighbourhood violence. *Urban Studies, 59*(14), 3005–3021. https://doi.org/10.1177/00420980211052149.

Sears, M. S., Repetti, R. L., Reynolds, B. M., Robles, T. F., & Krull, J. L. (2016). Spillover in the home: The effects of family conflict on parents' behavior. *Journal of Marriage and Family, 78*(1), 127–141. https://doi.org/10.1111/jomf.12265.

Sege, R. D., Amaya-Jackson, L., American Academy of Pediatrics Committee on Child Abuse and Neglect, et al. (2017). Clinical considerations related to the behavioral manifestations of child maltreatment. *Pediatrics, 139*(4), e20170100. https://doi.org/10.1542/peds.2017-0100.

Selye, H. (1956). *The Stress of Life*. McGraw-Hill.

Shaw, D. S., Dishion, T. J., Supplee, L., Gardner, F., & Arnds, K. (2006). Randomized trial of a family-centered approach to the prevention of early conduct problems: 2-year effects of the family check-up in early childhood. *Journal of Consulting and Clinical Psychology, 74*(1), 1–9. https://doi.org/10.1037/0022-006X.74.1.1.

Sheridan, M. A., Fox, N. A., Zeanah, C. H., McLaughlin, K. A., & Nelson III, C. A. (2012). Variation in neural development as a result of exposure to institutionalization early in childhood. *Proceedings of the National Academy of Sciences, 109*(32), 12927–12932.

Sheridan, M. A., & McLaughlin, K. A. (2014). Dimensions of early experience and neural development: Deprivation and threat. *Trends in Cognitive Sciences*, *18*(11), 580–585. https://doi.org/10.1016/j.tics.2014.09.001.

Sheridan, M. A., Peverill, M., Finn, A. S., & McLaughlin, K. A. (2017). Dimensions of childhood adversity have distinct associations with neural systems underlying executive functioning. *Development and Psychopathology*, *29*(5), 1777–1794. https://doi.org/10.1017/S0954579417001390.

Shetgiri, R. (2013). Bullying and victimization among children. *Advances in Pediatrics*, *60*(1), 33–51. https://doi.org/10.1016/j.yapd.2013.04.004.

Shonkoff, J. P., & Bales, S. N. (2011). Science does not speak for itself: Translating child development research for the public and its policymakers: Translating research for policymakers. *Child Development*, *82*(1), 17–32. https://doi.org/10.1111/j.1467-8624.2010.01538.x.

Shonkoff, J. P., & Fisher, P. A. (2013). Rethinking evidence-based practice and two-generation programs to create the future of early childhood policy. *Development and Psychopathology*, *25*(4pt2), 1635–1653. https://doi.org/10.1017/S0954579413000813.

Shonkoff, J. P., Garner, A. S., & The Committee on Psychosocial Aspects of Child and Family Health, Committee on Early Childhood, Adoption, and Dependent Care, and Section on Developmental and Behavioral Pediatrics. (2012). The lifelong effects of early childhood adversity and toxic stress. *Pediatrics*, *129*(1), e232–e246. https://doi.org/10.1542/peds.2011-2663.

Shonkoff, J. P., & Phillips, D. A. (2000). Promoting healthy development through intervention. In Shonkoff, J. P., & Phillips, D. A. (Eds.), *From Neurons to Neighborhoods: The Science of Early Childhood Development* (pp. 337–380). National Academies Press (US). www.ncbi.nlm.nih.gov/books/NBK225561/.

Shonkoff, J. P., Slopen, N., & Williams, D. R. (2021). Early Childhood adversity, toxic stress, and the impacts of racism on the foundations of health. *Annual Review of Public Health*, *42*(1), 115–134. https://doi.org/10.1146/annurev-publhealth-090419-101940.

Siegel, D. J. (2001). Toward an interpersonal neurobiology of the developing mind: Attachment relationships, "mindsight," and neural integration. *Infant Mental Health Journal*, *22*(1–2), 67–94. https://doi.org/10.1002/1097-0355(200101/04)22:1<67::AID-IMHJ3>3.0.CO;2-G.

Singh, G. K., & Kenney, M. K. (2013). Rising prevalence and neighborhood, social, and behavioral determinants of sleep problems in US children and adolescents, 2003–2012. *Sleep Disorders*, *2013*, 394320. https://doi.org/10.1155/2013/394320.

Skowron, E. A., Loken, E., Gatzke-Kopp, L. M., et al. (2011). Mapping cardiac physiology and parenting processes in maltreating mother–child dyads. *Journal of Family Psychology*, *25*(5), 663–674. https://doi.org/10.1037/a0024528.

Smider, N. A., Essex, M. J., Kalin, N. H., et al. (2002). Salivary cortisol as a predictor of socioemotional adjustment during kindergarten: A prospective study. *Child Development*, *73*(1), 75–92. https://doi.org/10.1111/1467-8624.00393.

Smith, J. D., Dishion, T. J., Shaw, D. S., et al. (2014). Coercive family process and early-onset conduct problems from age 2 to school entry. *Development and Psychopathology*, *26*(4 0 1), 917–932. https://doi.org/10.1017/S0954579414000169.

Smith, K. E., & Pollak, S. D. (2020). Rethinking concepts and categories for understanding the neurodevelopmental effects of childhood adversity. *Perspectives on Psychological Science*, *16*(1), 67–93. https://doi.org/10.1177/1745691620920725.

Smith, K. E., & Pollak, S. D. (2021). Social relationships and children's perceptions of adversity. *Child Development Perspectives*, *15*(4), 228–234. https://doi.org/10.1111/cdep.12427.

Sotardi, V. A. (2016). Understanding student stress and coping in elementary school: A mixed-method, longitudinal study. *Psychology in the Schools*, *53*(7), 705–721. https://doi.org/10.1002/pits.21938.

Spencer, M. B., Dupree, D., & Hartmann, T. (1997). A phenomenological variant of ecological systems theory (PVEST): A self-organization perspective in context. *Development and Psychopathology*, *9*(4), 817–833. https://doi.org/10.1017/s0954579497001454.

Stein, B. D., Jaycox, L. H., Kataoka, S. H., et al. (2003). A mental health intervention for schoolchildren exposed to violence a randomized controlled trial. *JAMA*, *290*(5), 603–611. https://doi.org/10.1001/jama.290.5.603.

Steinbeck, J. (1939). *The Grapes of Wrath*. The Viking Press.

Stempel, H., Cox-Martin, M., Bronsert, M., Dickinson, L. M., & Allison, M. A. (2017). Chronic school absenteeism and the role of adverse childhood experiences. *Academic Pediatrics*, *17*(8), 837–843. https://doi.org/10.1016/j.acap.2017.09.013.

Sterling, P., & Eyer, J. (1988). Allostasis: A new paradigm to explain arousal pathology. In S. Fisher & J. Reason (Eds.), *Handbook of Life Stress, Cognition and Health* (pp. 629–649). John Wiley & Sons.

Sternthal, M. J., Jun, H.-J., Earls, F., & Wright, R. J. (2010). Community violence and urban childhood asthma: A multilevel analysis. *European*

Respiratory Journal, 36(6), 1400–1409. https://doi.org/10.1183/09031936.00003010.

Sturge-Apple, M. L., Jacques, D. T., Davies, P. T., & Cicchetti, D. (2022). Maternal power assertive discipline and children's adjustment in high-risk families: A social domain theory approach. *Journal of Child and Family Studies, 31*(9), 2319–2330. https://doi.org/10.1007/s10826-021-02127-7.

Suchman, N. E., DeCoste, C., Castiglioni, N., et al. (2010). The mothers and toddlers program, an attachment-based parenting intervention for substance using women: Post-treatment results from a randomized clinical pilot. *Attachment & Human Development, 12*(5), 483–504. https://doi.org/10.1080/14616734.2010.501983.

Sumner, J. A., Colich, N. L., Uddin, M., Armstrong, D., & McLaughlin, K. A. (2019). Early experiences of threat, but not deprivation, are associated with accelerated biological aging in children and adolescents. *Biological Psychiatry, 85*(3), 268–278. https://doi.org/10.1016/j.biopsych.2018.09.008.

Szalacha, L. A., Erkut, S., Coll, C. G., et al. (2003). Discrimination and Puerto Rican children's and adolescents' mental health. *Cultural Diversity and Ethnic Minority Psychology, 9*(2), 141–155. https://doi.org/10.1037/1099-9809.9.2.141.

Szymanski, K., Sapanski, L., & Conway, F. (2011). Trauma and ADHD – association or diagnostic confusion? A clinical perspective. *Journal of Infant, Child, and Adolescent Psychotherapy, 10*(1), 51–59. https://doi.org/10.1080/15289168.2011.575704.

Tabachnick, A. R., Raby, K. L., Goldstein, A., Zajac, L., & Dozier, M. (2019). Effects of an attachment-based intervention in infancy on children's autonomic regulation during middle childhood. *Biological Psychology, 143*, 22–31. https://doi.org/10.1016/j.biopsycho.2019.01.006.

Taborsky, B., Kuijper, B., Fawcett, T. W., et al. (2022). An evolutionary perspective on stress responses, damage and repair. *Hormones and Behavior, 142*, 105180. https://doi.org/10.1016/j.yhbeh.2022.105180.

Takizawa, R., Maughan, B., & Arseneault, L. (2014). Adult health outcomes of childhood bullying victimization: Evidence from a five-decade longitudinal British birth cohort. *American Journal of Psychiatry, 171*(7), 777–784. https://doi.org/10.1176/appi.ajp.2014.13101401.

Tatum, B. D. (1997). *Why Are All the Black Kids Sitting Together in the Cafeteria? And Other Conversations about Race*. Basic Books.

Thakur, N., Hessler, D., Koita, K., et al. (2020). Pediatrics adverse childhood experiences and related life events screener (PEARLS) and health in a safety-net practice. *Child Abuse & Neglect, 108*, 104685. https://doi.org/10.1016/j.chiabu.2020.104685.

Theall, K. P., Shirtcliff, E. A., Dismukes, A. R., Wallace, M., & Drury, S. S. (2017). Association between neighborhood violence and biological stress in children. *JAMA Pediatrics*, *171*(1), 53. https://doi.org/10.1001/jamapediatrics.2016.2321.

Thomas, M. S., Crosby, S., & Vanderhaar, J. (2019). Trauma-informed practices in schools across two decades: An interdisciplinary review of research. *Review of Research in Education*, *43*(1), 422–452. https://doi.org/10.3102/0091732X18821123.

Thompson, R. A. (2014). Stress and child development. *The Future of Children*, *24*(1), 41–59.

Thompson, R. A., & Calkins, S. D. (1996). The double-edged sword: Emotional regulation for children at risk. *Development and Psychopathology*, *8*(1), 163–182. https://doi.org/10.1017/S0954579400007021.

Thomsen, M. R., Nayga, R. M., Alviola, P. A., & Rouse, H. L. (2016). The effect of food deserts on the body mass index of elementary school children. *American Journal of Agricultural Economics*, *98*(1), 1–18. https://doi.org/10.1093/ajae/aav039.

Thorvaldsen, S., Hansen, K. T., & Forsberg, J. T. (2024). Children and adolescents weathering the storm: Resilience in the presence of bullying victimization, harassment, and pandemic lockdown in northern Norway. *Scandinavian Journal of Psychology*, sjop.13012. https://doi.org/10.1111/sjop.13012.

Tillmann, S., Tobin, D., Avison, W., & Gilliland, J. (2018). Mental health benefits of interactions with nature in children and teenagers: A systematic review. *Journal of Epidemiology and Community Health*, *72*(10), 958–966. https://doi.org/10.1136/jech-2018-210436.

Tout, K., de Haan, M., Campbell, E. K., & Gunnar, M. R. (1998). Social behavior correlates of cortisol activity in child care: Gender differences and time-of-day effects. *Child Development*, *69*(5), 1247–1262. https://doi.org/10.1111/j.1467-8624.1998.tb06209.x.

Troop-Gordon, W., Sugimura, N., & Rudolph, K. D. (2017). Responses to interpersonal stress: Normative changes across childhood and the impact of peer victimization. *Child Development*, *88*(2), 640–657. https://doi.org/10.1111/cdev.12617.

Turner-Cobb, J. M., Rixon, L., & Jessop, D. S. (2008). A prospective study of diurnal cortisol responses to the social experience of school transition in four-year-old children: Anticipation, exposure, and adaptation. *Developmental Psychobiology*, *50*(4), 377–389. https://doi.org/10.1002/dev.20298.

Tyrrell, M. (2005). School phobia. *The Journal of School Nursing*, *21*(3), 147–151. https://doi.org/10.1177/10598405050210030401.

Ugarte, E., & Hastings, P. D. (2024). Assessing unpredictability in caregiver–child relationships: Insights from theoretical and empirical perspectives. *Development and Psychopathology*, *36*(3), 1070–1089. https://doi.org/10.1017/S0954579423000305.

Ungar, M., & Theron, L. (2020). Resilience and mental health: How multisystemic processes contribute to positive outcomes. *The Lancet Psychiatry*, *7*(5), 441–448. https://doi.org/10.1016/S2215-0366(19)30434-1.

Vaillancourt, T., Brittain, H., Krygsman, A., et al. (2021). School bullying before and during COVID-19: Results from a population-based randomized design. *Aggressive Behavior*, *47*(5), 557–569. https://doi.org/10.1002/ab.21986.

Vanaelst, B., De Vriendt, T., Huybrechts, I., Rinaldi, S., & De Henauw, S. (2012). Epidemiological approaches to measure childhood stress. *Paediatric and Perinatal Epidemiology*, *26*(3), 280–297. https://doi.org/10.1111/j.1365-3016.2012.01258.x.

Vélez, C. E., Wolchik, S. A., Tein, J.-Y., & Sandler, I. (2011). Protecting children from the consequences of divorce: A longitudinal study of the effects of parenting on children's coping processes. *Child Development*, *82*(1), 244–257. https://doi.org/10.1111/j.1467-8624.2010.01553.x.

Vermeer, H. J., & van IJzendoorn, M. H. (2006). Children's elevated cortisol levels at daycare: A review and meta-analysis. *Early Childhood Research Quarterly*, *21*(3), 390–401. https://doi.org/10.1016/j.ecresq.2006.07.004.

Walton, L. M. (2018). The effects of "bias based bullying" (BBB) on health, education, and cognitive–social–emotional outcomes in children with minority backgrounds: Proposed comprehensive public health intervention solutions. *Journal of Immigrant and Minority Health*, *20*(2), 492–496. https://doi.org/10.1007/s10903-017-0547-y.

Wang, X., & Maguire-Jack, K. (2018). Family and environmental influences on child behavioral health: The role of neighborhood disorder and adverse childhood experiences. *Journal of Developmental & Behavioral Pediatrics*, *39*(1), 28. https://doi.org/10.1097/DBP.0000000000000506.

Waters, S. F., West, T. V., & Mendes, W. B. (2014). Stress contagion: Physiological covariation between mothers and infants. *Psychological Science*, *25*(4), 934–942. https://doi.org/10.1177/0956797613518352.

Weatherston, D. J., Ribaudo, J., & Research, T. M. C. for I. M. H. (2020). The Michigan infant mental health home visiting model. *Infant Mental Health Journal*, *41*(2), 166–177. https://doi.org/10.1002/imhj.21838.

Weisz, J. R., & Kazdin, A. E. (2017). *Evidence-Based Psychotherapies for Children and Adolescents*: Third Edition. Guildford.

Wellman, H. M., & Woolley, J. D. (1990). From simple desires to ordinary beliefs: The early development of everyday psychology. *Cognition, 35*(3), 245–275. https://doi.org/10.1016/0010-0277(90)90024-E.

Wentzel, K., Russell, S., & Baker, S. (2009). Peer relationships and positive adjustment at school. In R. Gilman, E. S. Huebner, & M. J. Furlong (Eds.), *Handbook of Positive Psychology in Schools* (2nd ed.) (pp. 229–243). Routledge.

Whitaker, R. C., Dearth-Wesley, T., & Gooze, R. A. (2015). Workplace stress and the quality of teacher–children relationships in Head Start. *Early Childhood Research Quarterly, 30*, 57–69. https://doi.org/10.1016/j.ecresq.2014.08.008.

Williams, D. R., Lawrence, J. A., Davis, B. A., & Vu, C. (2019). Understanding how discrimination can affect health. *Health Services Research, 54*(S2), 1374–1388. https://doi.org/10.1111/1475-6773.13222.

Wolke, D., & Lereya, S. T. (2015). Long-term effects of bullying. *Archives of Disease in Childhood, 100*(9), 879–885. https://doi.org/10.1136/archdischild-2014-306667.

Wong, M. (2015). Voices of children, parents and teachers: How children cope with stress during school transition. *Early Child Development and Care, 185*(4), 658–678. https://doi.org/10.1080/03004430.2014.948872.

World Health Organization. (2019/2021). International classification of diseases, eleventh revision (ICD-11). https://icd.who.int/browse11. Licensed under Creative Commons Attribution-NoDerivatives 3.0 IGO licence (CC BY-ND 3.0 IGO).

Xu, Y., Harms, M. B., Green, C. S., Wilson, R. C., & Pollak, S. D. (2023). Childhood unpredictability and the development of exploration. *Proceedings of the National Academy of Sciences, 120*(49), e2303869120. https://doi.org/10.1073/pnas.2303869120.

Ye, M., Hessler, D., Ford, D., et al. (2023). Pediatric ACEs and related life event screener (PEARLS) latent domains and child health in a safety-net primary care practice. *BMC Pediatrics, 23*(1), 367. https://doi.org/10.1186/s12887-023-04163-2.

Zahn–Waxler, C., Klimes–Dougan, B., & Slattery, M. J. (2000). Internalizing problems of childhood and adolescence: Prospects, pitfalls, and progress in understanding the development of anxiety and depression. *Development and Psychopathology, 12*(3), 443–466. https://doi.org/10.1017/S0954579400003102.

Zhu, Y. (2023). "Big brothers and sisters have my back": Benefits and risks of befriending older peers as a strategy to deal with school bullying. *Child Abuse Review, 32*(3), e2827. https://doi.org/10.1002/car.2827.

Zietz, S., Lansford, J. E., Liu, Q., et al. (2022). A longitudinal examination of the family stress model of economic hardship in seven countries. *Children and Youth Services Review, 143*, 106661. https://doi.org/10.1016/j.childyouth.2022.106661.

Zinsser, K. M., Bailey, C. S., Curby, T. W., Denham, S. A., & Bassett, H. H. (2013). Exploring the predictable classroom: Preschool teacher stress, emotional supportiveness, and students' social-emotional behavior in private and Head Start classrooms. *HS Dialog, 16*(2), Article 2. https://doi.org/10.55370/hsdialog.v16i2.95.

Cambridge Elements

Child Development

Marc H. Bornstein
National Institute of Child Health and Human Development, Bethesda
Institute for Fiscal Studies, London
UNICEF, New York City

Marc H. Bornstein is an Affiliate of the *Eunice Kennedy Shriver* National Institute of Child Health and Human Development, an International Research Fellow at the Institute for Fiscal Studies (London), and UNICEF Senior Advisor for Research for ECD Parenting Programmes. Bornstein is President Emeritus of the Society for Research in *Child Development*, Editor Emeritus of Child Development, and founding Editor of *Parenting: Science and Practice*.

About the Series

Child development is a lively and engaging, yet serious and real-world subject of scientific study that encompasses myriad theories, methods, substantive areas, and applied concerns. Cambridge Elements in Child Development addresses many contemporary topics in child development with unique, comprehensive, and state-of-the-art treatments of principal issues, primary currents of thinking, original perspectives, and empirical contributions to understanding early human development.

Cambridge Elements

Child Development

Elements in the Series

Autobiographical Memory and Narrative in Childhood
Robyn Fivush

Children and Climate Change
Ann V. Sanson, Karina Padilla Malca, Judith Van Hoorn and Susie Burke

Socialization and Socioemotional Development in Chinese Children
Xinyin Chen

Giftedness in Childhood
Robert J. Sternberg and Ophélie A. Desmet

The Adopted Child
David Brodzinsky and Jesus Palacios

Early Childhood and Digital Media
Rachel Barr, Heather Kirkorian, Sarah Coyne and Jenny Radesky

Equity for Children in the United States
Shantel Meek, Evandra Catherine, Xigrid Soto-Boykin and Darielle Blevins

Children's Defensive Mindset
Kenneth A. Dodge

Temperament and Child Development in Context
Liliana J. Lengua, Maria A. Gartstein, Qing Zhou, Craig R. Colder and Debrielle T. Jacques

Life History and Child Development
Lei Chang and Hui Jing Lu

Theory of Mind in Childhood
Diane Poulin-Dubois

Stress in Childhood
Camelia E. Hostinar, Anna M. Parenteau, Geneva M. Jost, Sally Hang, Joanna Y. Guan, and Jamie M. Lawler

A full series listing is available at: www.cambridge.org/EICD

For EU product safety concerns, contact us at Calle de José Abascal, 56–1°, 28003 Madrid, Spain or eugpsr@cambridge.org.

www.ingramcontent.com/pod-product-compliance
Lightning Source LLC
LaVergne TN
LVHW011848060526
838200LV00054B/4226